Contents

Easy chocolate fudge cake 6
Easy carrot cake 7
Easy blueberry muffins 8
Easy chocolate cake 9
Easy teriyaki chicken 11
Easy millionaire's shortbread 11
Easy coronation chicken 13
Easy rocky road 13
Easy banana muffins 14
Easy bread rolls 15
Easy chicken fajitas 16
Easy chocolate biscuits 18
Easy chicken curry 19
Easy crêpes 20
Easy cornflake tart 21
Easy caramel cake 22
Easy chocolate molten cakes 23
Easy vegan pancakes 24
Easy banana pancakes 25
Easy Singapore noodles 26
Easy onion bhajis 27
Easy honey flapjacks 28
Easy steak pie 28
Easy chocolate chip cookies 29
Easy banoffee pie 30
Easy beef burritos 31
Easy soda bread 32
Easy butter chicken 33
Easy jam tarts 34
Easy salad dressing 35
Easy chocolate bark 35

- Easy egg muffins ... 36
- Easy gravy ... 37
- Easy piccalilli ... 37
- Easy beef in black bean sauce ... 38
- Easy green vegetable soup ... 39
- Easy caponata stew ... 40
- Easy chicken burritos ... 41
- Easy breakfast burritos ... 42
- Easy vegan tacos ... 44
- Easy cheesy mustard toad-in-the-hole with broccoli ... 45
- Easy vegan pho ... 46
- Easy soup maker lentil soup ... 47
- Easy vanilla cupcakes ... 48
- Easy pound cake ... 49
- Easy pancakes ... 49
- Easy chicken stew ... 50
- Easy-to-scale cheesy fish pie with kale ... 51
- Easy sausage & courgette pilaf ... 52
- Easy chocolate mousse ... 53
- Easy slow cooker chicken casserole ... 54
- Easy moussaka ... 55
- Easy vegan chocolate cake ... 56
- Easy iced tea ... 58
- Easy classic lasagne ... 59
- Easy-peasy fruitcake ... 60
- Easy sweet & sour chicken ... 61
- Easy Easter biscuits ... 62
- Easy spaghetti Bolognese ... 63
- Easy falafels ... 63
- Super-easy birthday cake ... 65
- Easy huevos rancheros ... 66
- Unbelievably easy mince pies ... 66
- Strawberry cheesecake in 4 easy steps ... 67

Easy bibimbap	69
Easy smoked turkey crown	70
Really easy roasted red pepper sauce	71
Easy sausage & fennel risotto	72
Easy sangria	73
Easy slow cooker lamb curry	73
Really easy cinnamon rolls	74
Family meals: Easy fish pie recipe	75
Super-easy sausage casserole	77
Easy pulled beef ragu	77
Easy soup maker roast chicken soup	78
Easy salmon coulibiac	79
Easy lamb hotpot	80
Easy chicken & chickpea tagine	81
Easy pesto lasagne	82
Easy meatloaf with spaghetti & tomato sauce	83
Quick & easy tiramisu	84
Easy sourdough bread	85
Easy falafel burgers	86
Easy lentil pastries	87
Easy flatbread	88
Easy turkey crown	88
Easy creamy coleslaw	89
Easy creamed spinach	90
Easy fruitcake	90
Easy risotto with bacon & peas	91
Easy mackerel bowls	92
Easy brownies	93
Easy yogurt flatbreads	94
Easy hummus recipe	95
Easy cherry jam	95
Easy lemon muffins	96
Easy paella	97

Super-easy fruit ice cream	98
Easy ratatouille	99
Easy Christmas turkey	99
Easy one-pot chicken casserole	101
Easy Thai prawn curry	102
Easy chilli con carne	102
Pizza Margherita in 4 easy steps	103
Easy fluffy scones	105
Easy vanilla cake	106
Easy treacle sponge	107
Easy chicken gumbo	108
Easy Eccles cakes	109
Easy meatballs	110
Quiche Lorraine in 4 easy steps	112
Easy Scotch eggs	114
Easy roast beef	115
Easy-bake bread	116
Family meals: Easy lamb tagine	117
Really easy roast chicken	118
Bread in four easy steps	120
Cheese soufflé in 4 easy steps	121
Easy chocolate brownie cake	123
Easy chicken casserole	124
Easy raspberry & ginger trifle cheesecake	124
Easy biscotti	125
Really easy lemonade	126
Easy meatloaf recipe	127
Easy Christmas pudding ice cream	128
Easy Easter nests	128
Easy apple fruit cake	129
Easy baked pears with amaretti	130
Easy white bread	131
Easy beef hotpot	132

- Easy Thai green chicken curry 133
- Easy turkey paella 134
- Easy turkey paella 134
- Easy lentil curry 135
- Easy garlic sauce 136
- Easy homemade chocolate bark 137
- Easy chicken tagine 138
- Family meals: Easy beef stew with sweet potato topping 139
- Easy peasy risotto with chilli & mint crumbs 140
- Really easy cheese fondue 141
- Easy cheese & onion slice 141
- Easy ratatouille with poached eggs 142
- Quick & easy party nibbles 143
- Easy elderflower liqueur 145

Easy chocolate fudge cake

Prep: 25 mins **Cook:** 30 mins

Easy

Serves 8

Ingredients

- 150ml sunflower oil, plus extra for the tin
- 175g self-raising flour
- 2 tbsp cocoa powder
- 1 tsp bicarbonate of soda
- 150g caster sugar
- 2 tbsp golden syrup
- 2 large eggs, lightly beaten
- 150ml semi-skimmed milk

For the icing

- 100g unsalted butter
- 225g icing sugar
- 40g cocoa powder
- 2½ tbsp milk (a little more if needed)

Method

STEP 1

Heat the oven to 180C/160C fan/gas 4. Oil and line the base of two 18cm sandwich tins. Sieve the flour, cocoa powder and bicarbonate of soda into a bowl. Add the caster sugar and mix well.

STEP 2

Make a well in the centre and add the golden syrup, eggs, sunflower oil and milk. Beat well with an electric whisk until smooth.

STEP 3

Pour the mixture into the two tins and bake for 25-30 mins until risen and firm to the touch. Remove from oven, leave to cool for 10 mins before turning out onto a cooling rack.

STEP 4

To make the icing, beat the unsalted butter in a bowl until soft. Gradually sieve and beat in the icing sugar and cocoa powder, then add enough of the milk to make the icing fluffy and spreadable.

STEP 5

Sandwich the two cakes together with the butter icing and cover the sides and the top of the cake with more icing.

Easy carrot cake

Prep: 35 mins **Cook:** 30 mins

Plus cooling

Easy

Serves 10-12

Ingredients

- 230ml vegetable oil, plus extra for the tin
- 100g natural yogurt
- 4 large eggs
- 1½ tsp vanilla extract
- ½ orange, zested
- 265g self-raising flour
- 335g light muscovado sugar
- 2½ tsp ground cinnamon
- ¼ fresh nutmeg, finely grated
- 265g carrots (about 3), grated
- 100g sultanas or raisins
- 100g walnuts or pecans, roughly chopped (optional)

For the icing

- 100g slightly salted butter, softened
- 300g icing sugar
- 100g soft cheese

Method

STEP 1

Heat the oven to 180C/160C fan/gas 4. Oil and line the base and sides of two 20cm cake tins with baking parchment. Whisk the oil, yogurt, eggs, vanilla and zest in a jug. Mix the flour, sugar, cinnamon and nutmeg with a good pinch of salt in a bowl. Squeeze any lumps of sugar through your fingers, shaking the bowl a few times to bring the lumps to the surface.

STEP 2

Add the wet ingredients to the dry, along with the carrots, raisins and half the nuts, if using. Mix well to combine, then divide between the tins.

STEP 3

Bake for 25-30 mins or until a skewer inserted into the centre of the cake comes out clean. If any wet mixture clings to the skewer, return to the oven for 5 mins, then check again. Leave to cool in the tins.

STEP 4

To make the icing, beat the butter and sugar together until smooth. Add half the soft cheese and beat again, then add the rest (adding it bit by bit prevents the icing from splitting). Remove the cakes from the tins and sandwich together with half the icing. Top with the remaining icing and scatter with the remaining walnuts. *Will keep in the fridge for up to five days.* Best eaten at room temperature.

Easy blueberry muffins

Prep: 20 mins **Cook:** 20 mins

Easy

Makes 12

Ingredients

- 100g unsalted butter softened, plus 1 tbsp, melted, for greasing
- 140g golden caster sugar
- 2 large eggs
- 140g natural yogurt
- 1 tsp vanilla extract
- 2 tbsp milk
- 250g plain flour
- 2 tsp baking powder
- 1 tsp bicarbonate of soda
- 125g pack blueberries (or use frozen)

Method

STEP 1

Heat oven to 200C/180C fan/gas 6 and line a 12-hole muffin tin with paper cases. Beat the butter and caster sugar together until pale and fluffy. Add the eggs and beat in for 1 min, then mix in the yogurt, vanilla extract and milk. Combine the flour, baking powder and bicarb in a bowl with ¼ tsp fine salt, then tip this into the wet ingredients and stir in. Finally, fold in the blueberries and divide the mixture between the muffin cases.

STEP 2

Bake for 5 mins, then reduce oven to 180C/160C fan/gas 4 and bake for 15-18 mins more until risen and golden, and a cocktail stick inserted into the centre comes out clean.

STEP 3

Cool in the tin for 10 mins, then carefully lift out onto a wire rack to finish cooling. Will keep for 3-4 days in an airtight container – after a day or two, pop them in the microwave for 10-15 secs on high to freshen up.

Easy chocolate cake

Prep: 35 mins **Cook:** 20 mins

Easy

Serves 12 - 14

Ingredients

For the cake

- 200g golden caster sugar
- 200g unsalted butter, softened plus extra for the tins
- 4 large eggs
- 200g self-raising flour
- 2 tbsp cocoa powder
- 1 tsp baking powder
- ½ tsp vanilla extract
- 2 tbsp milk

For the buttercream

- 100g milk chocolate, chopped
- 200g butter, softened
- 400g icing sugar
- 5 tbsp cocoa powder
- 2 tbsp milk

For the chocolate shards (optional)

- 50g dark chocolate
- 25g milk chocolate
- 25g white chocolate

Method

STEP 1

Heat oven to 190C/170C fan/gas 5. Butter the base and sides of two 20cm round sandwich tins and line the bases with baking parchment.

STEP 2

In a large bowl, beat together 200g golden caster sugar, 200g softened unsalted butter, 4 large eggs, 200g self-raising flour, 2 tbsp cocoa powder, 1 tsp baking powder, ½ tsp vanilla extract, 2 tbsp milk and a pinch of salt until pale.

STEP 3

Divide the mixture between the prepared tins. Bake for 20 mins or until a skewer inserted into the centre of the cake comes out clean.

STEP 4

Leave to cool in the tin for 10 mins, then turn out onto a wire rack to cool completely.

STEP 5

For the buttercream, put 100g chopped milk chocolate in a heatproof bowl and melt in the microwave, stirring every 30 secs. Leave the melted chocolate to cool for 5 mins.

STEP 6

Mash 200g softened butter and 400g icing sugar together with a fork, then switch to a wooden spoon or electric beaters, if you have them.

STEP 7

Sift in 5 tbsp cocoa powder with a pinch of salt and pour in the melted chocolate and 2 tbsp milk. Mix again until smooth.

STEP 8

On a cake stand or large plate, sandwich the cakes together with half of the buttercream, then spread the rest on top. Decorate with chocolate shards, if you like.

STEP 9

To make chocolate shards: melt 50g dark chocolate and pour it onto a tray lined with baking parchment or foil.

STEP 10

Now melt 25g milk chocolate and 25g white chocolate and drizzle them over the dark chocolate before it sets.

STEP 11

Shake the tray gently to level the mixture then leave to set somewhere cool. Chop into shards.

Easy teriyaki chicken

Prep: 5 mins **Cook:** 15 mins

Easy

Serves 4

Ingredients

- 2 tbsp toasted sesame oil
- 6 skinless and boneless chicken thighs, sliced
- 2 large garlic cloves, crushed
- 1 thumb-sized piece ginger, grated
- 50g runny honey
- 30ml light soy sauce
- 1 tbsp rice wine vinegar
- 1 tbsp sesame seeds, to serve
- 4 spring onions, shredded, to serve
- sticky rice, to serve
- steamed bok choi or spring greens, to serve

Method

STEP 1

Heat the oil in a non-stick pan over a medium heat. Add the chicken and fry for 7 mins, or until golden. Add the garlic and ginger and fry for 2 mins. Stir in the honey, soy sauce, vinegar and 100ml water. Bring to the boil and cook for 2 - 5 mins over a medium heat until the chicken is sticky and coated in a thick sauce.

STEP 2

Scatter over the spring onions and sesame seeds, then serve the chicken with the rice and steamed veg.

Easy millionaire's shortbread

Prep: 25 mins **Cook:** 35 mins

Easy

Makes up to 24 squares

Ingredients

For the shortbread

- 250g plain flour
- 75g caster sugar

- 175g butter, softened

For the caramel

- 100g butter or margarine
- 100g light muscovado sugar
- 397g can condensed milk

For the topping

- 200g plain or milk chocolate, broken into pieces

Method

STEP 1

Heat the oven to 180C/160C fan/gas 4. Lightly grease and line a 20-22cm square or rectangular baking tin with a lip of at least 3cm.

STEP 2

To make the shortbread, mix 250g plain flour and 75g caster sugar in a bowl. Rub in 175g softened butter until the mixture resembles fine breadcrumbs.

STEP 3

Knead the mixture together until it forms a dough, then press into the base of the prepared tin.

STEP 4

Prick the shortbread lightly with a fork and bake for 20 minutes or until firm to the touch and very lightly browned. Leave to cool in the tin.

STEP 5

To make the caramel, place 100g butter or margarine, 100g light muscovado sugar and the can of condensed milk in a pan and heat gently until the sugar has dissolved. Continually stir with a spatula to make sure no sugar sticks to the bottom of the pan. (This can leave brown specks in the caramel but won't affect the flavour.)

STEP 6

Turn up the heat to medium high, stirring all the time, and bring to the boil, then lower the heat back to low and stirring continuously, for about 5-10 minutes or until the mixture has thickened slightly. Pour over the shortbread and leave to cool.

STEP 7

For the topping, melt 200g plain or milk chocolate slowly in a bowl over a pan of hot water. Pour over the cold caramel and leave to set. Cut into squares or bars with a hot knife.

Easy coronation chicken

Prep: 5 mins

No cook

Easy

Serves 4-6

Ingredients

- 6 tbsp mayonnaise
- 2-3 tsp mild curry powder, to taste
- ½ tsp ground cinnamon
- 2 tbsp mango chutney
- 1-3 tbsp sultanas, or to taste
- 500g shredded cooked chicken

Method

STEP 1

Mix the mayo, curry powder, cinnamon, chutney and sultanas together and season with black pepper.

STEP 2

Add the shredded chicken and stir to coat in the sauce. Stir in 2 tbsp water to loosen if needed, then season and serve as desired.

Easy rocky road

Prep: 15 mins **Cook:** 5 mins

plus chilling

Easy

Serves 12

Ingredients

- 200g digestive biscuits (Rich Tea can also be used)
- 135g butter or margarine

- 200g dark chocolate (70% cocoa works best)
- 2-3 tbsp golden syrup

Optional (up to 100g)

- raisins, dried cranberries or any dried fruit
- nuts
- 100g mini marshmallows (chopped regular marshmallows work too)
- icing sugar, to dust
- popcorn
- honeycomb, broken into pieces

Method

STEP 1

Grease and line an 18cm square brownie tin with baking paper.

STEP 2

Place 200g digestive biscuits in a freezer bag and bash with a rolling pin or just the side of your fist until they're broken into a mixture of everything between dust and 50p-sized lumps. Set aside.

STEP 3

In a large saucepan melt 135g butter or margarine, 200g dark chocolate and 2-3 tbsp golden syrup over a gentle heat stirring constantly until there are no or almost no more lumps of chocolate visible, then remove from the heat. Leave to cool.

STEP 4

Take the biscuits, 100g mini marshmallows and up to 100g of additional ingredients (dried fruit, nuts, popcorn, honeycomb), if you like, and stir into the chocolate mixture until everything is completely covered.

STEP 5

Tip the mixture into the lined baking tin, and spread it out to the corners. Chill for at least 2 hrs then dust with icing sugar and cut into 12 fingers.

Easy banana muffins

Prep: 15 mins **Cook:** 25 mins

Easy

Makes 12

Ingredients

- 250g self-raising flour
- 1 tsp baking powder
- ½ tsp bicarbonate of soda
- 110g caster sugar
- 75g butter, melted
- 1 tsp vanilla extract
- 2 eggs
- 2 large ripe bananas, mashed
- 125ml buttermilk (or add 1 tsp of lemon juice to milk and leave for 20 mins)
- 50g pecans, chopped, plus extra to decorate (optional)

Method

STEP 1

Heat the oven to 190C/170C Fan/gas 5. Line a 12-hole muffin tin with paper cases. Sift together the flour, baking powder, bicarbonate of soda and caster sugar with a big pinch of salt. In a separate bowl mix the melted butter, vanilla extract, eggs, mashed bananas and buttermilk.

STEP 2

Make a well in the centre of the dry ingredients and pour the wet ingredients in. Roughly mix together with a fork, being careful not to over-mix. Scatter in the chopped pecans, if using, then spoon the mixture into the muffin cases. Top with pecan halves, then bake for 20-25 mins, until golden brown. Cool on a wire rack.

Easy bread rolls

Prep: 30 mins **Cook:** 25 mins - 30 mins

Easy

Makes 8

Ingredients

- 500g strong white bread flour, plus extra for dusting
- 7g sachet fast action yeast
- 1 tsp white caster sugar
- 2 tsp fine salt
- 1 tsp sunflower oil, plus extra for the work surface and bowl

Method

STEP 1

Tip the flour, yeast, sugar, salt and oil into a bowl. Pour over 325ml warm water, then mix (with a spatula or your hand), until it comes together as a shaggy dough. Make sure all the flour has been incorporated. Cover and leave for 10 mins.

STEP 2

Lightly oil your work surface and tip the dough onto it. Knead the dough for at least 10 mins until it becomes tighter and springy – if you have a stand mixer you can do this with a dough hook for 5 mins. Pull the dough into a ball and put in a clean, oiled bowl. Leave for 1 hr, or until doubled in size.

STEP 3

Tip the dough onto a lightly floured surface and roll into a long sausage shape. Halve the dough, then divide each half into four pieces, so you have eight equal-sized portions. Roll each into a tight ball and put on a dusted baking tray, leaving some room between each ball for rising. Cover with a damp tea towel and leave in a warm place to prove for 40 mins-1 hr or until almost doubled in size.

STEP 4

Heat the oven to 230C/210C fan/gas 8. When the dough is ready, dust each ball with a bit more flour. (If you like, you can glaze the rolls with milk or beaten egg, and top with seeds.) Bake for 25-30mins, until light brown and hollow sounding when tapped on the base. Leave to cool on a wire rack.

RECIPE TIPS

ADJUST PORTIONS

This recipe makes smallish rolls but can easily be adjusted. For burger buns, divide the mix into six instead of eight, or for hotdog buns, roll them into finger shapes instead of balls.

MAKE IT WHOLEMEAL

For wholemeal rolls, use 250g white flour and 250g of wholemeal flour.

Easy chicken fajitas

Prep: 15 mins **Cook:** 10 mins

Easy

Serves 3

Ingredients

- 2 large chicken breasts, finely sliced
- 1 red onion, finely sliced
- 1 red pepper, sliced
- 1 red chilli, finely sliced (optional)

For the marinade

- 1 heaped tbsp smoked paprika
- 1 tbsp ground coriander
- pinch of ground cumin
- 2 medium garlic cloves, crushed
- 4 tbsp olive oil
- 1 lime, juiced
- 4-5 drops Tabasco

To serve

- 6 medium tortillas
- bag mixed salad
- 230g tub fresh salsa

Method

STEP 1

Heat oven to 200C/180C fan/gas 6 and wrap 6 medium tortillas in foil.

STEP 2

Mix 1 heaped tbsp smoked paprika, 1 tbsp ground coriander, a pinch of ground cumin, 2 crushed garlic cloves, 4 tbsp olive oil, the juice of 1 lime and 4-5 drops Tabasco together in a bowl with a big pinch each of salt and pepper.

STEP 3

Stir 2 finely sliced chicken breasts, 1 finely sliced red onion, 1 sliced red pepper and 1 finely sliced red chilli, if using, into the marinade.

STEP 4

Heat a griddle pan until smoking hot and add the chicken and marinade to the pan.

STEP 5

Keep everything moving over a high heat for about 5 mins using tongs until you get a nice charred effect. If your griddle pan is small you may need to do this in two batches.

STEP 6

To check the chicken is cooked, find the thickest part and tear in half – if any part is still raw cook until done.

STEP 7

Put the tortillas in the oven to heat up and serve with the cooked chicken, a bag of mixed salad and one 230g tub of fresh salsa.

Easy chocolate biscuits

Prep: 25 mins **Cook:** 10 mins - 15 mins

Easy

Makes 25 biscuits

Ingredients

- 250g butter, softened
- 350g light soft brown sugar
- 2 large eggs
- 350g self-raising flour
- 100g cocoa powder
- 200g chocolate chips or chopped chocolate chunks, or 400g for optional dipping (choose your favourite type)

Method

STEP 1

Beat the butter and sugar together with an optional pinch of sea salt in a bowl until light and fluffy, then beat in the eggs one at a time. Sift over the flour and cocoa powder and beat into the butter mix, then fold through the chocolate chips. The mix can be made up to 2 days ahead and chilled or frozen for a month, or used straight away.

STEP 2

To bake, heat oven to 190C/170C fan/gas 5. If the mix is at room temperature, place evenly spaced spoonfuls on parchment-lined baking sheets, allowing 2 tbsp for each cookie. If the mix is fridge cold, you can roll it into 40g balls before baking. The balls can be frozen and the biscuits baked from frozen, but they'll need a few minutes more. Bake for 12-15 mins until spread out and crusty around the outside. Leave to cool slightly and enjoy warm, or leave to cool completely and eat cold. The biscuits will keep in a tin for three days.

STEP 3

As an optional extra, the biscuits can be dipped in chocolate. To do this, melt your chosen type of chocolate in a bowl over a pan of simmering water or in the microwave. Leave to cool a little, then dip half of each biscuit in the chocolate and leave them on parchment-lined trays somewhere cool to set. Again, the dipped biscuits will keep for up to three days in a tin or lidded plastic container.

RECIPE TIPS

ADD YOUR FAVOURITE BITS

Use the easy recipe as a blueprint for adding any of your favourite biscuit bits. Any chopped nuts or bits of toffee, honeycomb or chopped dried fruit would work well.

GIVE YOUR BISCUITS A 'FLORENTINE' FINISH

After dipping you can give the biscuits a 'Florentine' finish by scattering the wet warm chocolate with flaked almonds or chopped pistachios or bits of dried fruit.

Easy chicken curry

Prep: 5 mins **Cook:** 45 mins

Easy

Serves 4

Ingredients

- 2 tbsp sunflower oil
- 1 onion, thinly sliced
- 2 garlic cloves, crushed
- thumb-sized piece of ginger, grated
- 6 chicken thighs, boneless and skinless
- 3 tbsp medium spice paste (tikka works well)
- 400g can chopped tomatoes
- 100g Greek yogurt
- 1 small bunch of coriander, leaves chopped
- 50g ground almonds
- naan breads or cooked basmati rice, to serve

Method

STEP 1

Heat the oil in a flameproof casserole dish or large frying pan over a medium heat. Add the onion and a generous pinch of salt and fry for 8-10 mins, or until the onion has turned golden brown and sticky. Add the garlic and ginger, cooking for a further minute.

STEP 2

Chop the chicken into chunky 3cm pieces, add to the pan and fry for 5 mins before stirring through the spice paste and tomatoes, along with 250ml water. Bring to the boil, lower to a simmer and cook on a gentle heat uncovered for 25-30 mins or until rich and slightly reduced. Stir though the yogurt, coriander and ground almonds, season and serve with warm naan or fluffy basmati rice.

Easy crêpes

Prep: 5 mins **Cook:** 20 mins

plus resting

Easy

Makes 8 large pancakes

Ingredients

- 175g plain flour
- 3 large eggs
- 450ml milk
- sunflower oil, for frying

Method

STEP 1

Weigh the flour in a large jug or bowl. Crack in the eggs, add half the milk and a pinch of salt. Whisk to a smooth, thick batter. Add the remaining milk and whisk again. Set aside for at least 30 mins.

STEP 2

Heat a large non-stick crêpe pan or frying pan. Add a drizzle of oil, then wipe out the excess with kitchen paper. When the pan is hot, add enough batter to just cover the surface, swirling it and pouring any excess back into the bowl. The pancake should be as thin as possible. When the edges are peeling away from the sides of the pan, shake it to see if the pancake easily releases and is browning on the underside. If not, cook a little longer. Flip and cook the other side for a minute or two. Serve, or keep warm in a low oven.

RECIPE TIPS

MAKE-AHEAD

The pancake batter will keep in the fridge for up to one day.

Easy cornflake tart

Prep: 20 mins **Cook:** 40 mins

Easy

Serves 8-10

Ingredients

- 320g ready-rolled shortcrust pastry
- plain flour, to dust
- 50g butter
- 125g golden syrup
- 25g light brown soft sugar
- 100g cornflakes
- 125g strawberry or raspberry jam
- custard, to serve

Method

STEP 1

Heat the oven to 180C/160C fan/gas 4. Unroll the pastry and briefly roll out on a lightly floured work surface until it's large enough to fit a 23cm loose-bottomed tart tin. Use the rolling pin to lift the pastry over the tin, then press into the corners and sides so the excess pastry hangs over the rim. Trim this away, leaving just a small amount of excess hanging over the rim.

STEP 2

Line the pastry with baking parchment and fill with baking beans or uncooked rice. Bake for 15 mins. Remove the parchment and beans, then bake for another 5-10 mins until just golden. Remove from the oven and trim any excess pastry from the edges using a serrated knife.

STEP 3

Heat the butter, syrup and sugar in a small pan with a pinch of salt, stirring frequently, until melted and smooth. Fold in the cornflakes to coat in the butter mixture.

STEP 4

Spoon the jam into the cooked pastry base, then level the surface. Tip the cornflake mixture over the jam and gently press down until all of the jam is covered with a layer of the mixture. Return the tart to the oven and bake for another 5 mins until the cornflakes are golden and toasted. Leave to cool until just warm before slicing and serving with custard.

Easy caramel cake

Prep: 30 mins **Cook:** 30 mins

Plus cooling

Easy

Serves 12-14

Ingredients

- 225g softened salted butter, plus extra for the tins
- 125g golden caster sugar
- 100g light brown soft sugar
- 1 tsp vanilla extract
- 4 large eggs
- 225g self raising flour
- 2 tbsp milk
- toffee, chocolate or caramel pieces, to decorate
- For the icing
- 200g softened salted butter
- 400g icing sugar (golden icing sugar if you can find it – it adds a golden colour and caramel flavour)
- 70g caramel sauce, dulce de leche or caramel spread, plus 3 tbsp to serve

Method

STEP 1

Heat the oven to 180C/160C fan/gas 4. Butter two 20cm springform tins and line the bases with baking parchment.

STEP 2

Beat the butter and both sugars in a bowl with an electric whisk for a few mins until lighter in colour and fluffy. Add the vanilla and the eggs, one at a time, adding a spoonful of flour and beating in between each egg. Add the remaining flour and milk. Divide between the cake tins and bake for 25-30 mins until they're golden, spring back when pressed, and a skewer comes out clean when inserted into the middle. Cool in the tins for a few mins, then tip out and leave to cool completely on a wire rack.

STEP 3

Meanwhile, for the icing, put the butter and icing sugar in a bowl and whisk for a few mins until light and airy. Whisk in the caramel briefly, adding 1 tbsp of boiling water to loosen, if needed. Set aside until the sponges are completely cool before assembling, or the icing will melt.

STEP 4

Use half the icing to sandwich the cakes together, then spread the remainder over the top, smoothing it out with a knife or the back of a spoon. Leave in a cool place until ready to serve. Drizzle with the 3 tbsp extra sauce (warm briefly in the microwave if it's a little stiff), allowing some to drip down the sides if you like, and scatter over the toffee, chocolate or caramel pieces to serve. Edible glitter, birthday candles or sparklers, optional.

RECIPE TIPS

TRY CHOCOLATE

For chocolate lovers, add 3 tbsp cocoa to the cake batter and drizzle over melted and cooled chocolate instead of more caramel. You could also top with chopped nuts, sprinkles or edible flowers depending on who you're making it for.

Easy chocolate molten cakes

Prep: 15 mins **Cook:** 20 mins

Easy

Makes 6

Ingredients

- 100g butter, plus extra to grease
- 100g dark chocolate, chopped
- 150g light brown soft sugar
- 3 large eggs
- ½ tsp vanilla extract
- 50g plain flour
- single cream, to serve

Method

STEP 1

Heat oven to 200C/180C fan/gas 6. Butter 6 dariole moulds or basins well and place on a baking tray.

STEP 2

Put 100g butter and 100g chopped dark chocolate in a heatproof bowl and set over a pan of hot water (or alternatively put in the microwave and melt in 30 second bursts on a low setting) and stir until smooth. Set aside to cool slightly for 15 mins.

STEP 3

Using an electric hand whisk, mix in 150g light brown soft sugar, then 3 large eggs, one at a time, followed by ½ tsp vanilla extract and finally 50g plain flour. Divide the mixture among the darioles or basins.

STEP 4

You can now either put the mixture in the fridge, or freezer until you're ready to bake them. Can be cooked straight from frozen for 16 mins, or bake now for 10-12 mins until the tops are firm to the touch but the middles still feel squidgy.

STEP 5

Carefully run a knife around the edge of each pudding, then turn out onto serving plates and serve with single cream.

Easy vegan pancakes

Prep: 5 mins **Cook:** 30 mins

Easy

Serves 4-6 (makes 16 pancakes)

Ingredients

- 300g self-raising flour
- 1 tsp baking powder
- 1 tbsp sugar (any kind)
- 1 tbsp vanilla extract
- 400ml plant-based milk (such as oat, almond or soya)
- 1 tbsp vegetable oil for cooking

To serve (optional)

- banana slices, blueberries, maple syrup, vegan chocolate chips, plant-based yogurt

Method

STEP 1

Whisk the flour, baking powder, sugar, vanilla extract and a pinch of salt in a bowl using a balloon whisk until mixed. Slowly pour in the milk until you get a smooth, thick batter.

STEP 2

Heat a little of the oil in a non-stick frying pan over a medium-low heat, and add 2 tbsp batter into the pan at a time to make small, round pancakes. You will need to do this in batches of two-three at a time. Cook for 3-4 mins until the edges are set, and bubbles are appearing on the surface. Flip the pancakes over and cook for another 2-3 mins until golden on both sides and cooked through. Keep warm in a low oven while you cook the remaining pancakes.

STEP 3

Serve stacked with lots of toppings of your choice, or serve with bowls of toppings for everyone to help themselves.

Easy banana pancakes

Prep: 5 mins **Cook:** 10 mins

Easy

Makes 12 pancakes

Ingredients

- 350g self-raising flour
- 1 tsp baking powder
- 2 very ripe bananas
- 2 medium eggs
- 1 tsp vanilla extract
- 250ml whole milk
- butter, for frying

To serve

- 2 just ripe bananas, sliced
- maple syrup (optional)
- pecan halves, toasted and roughly chopped (optional)

Method

STEP 1

Sieve the flour, baking powder and a generous pinch of salt into a large bowl. In a separate mixing bowl, mash the very ripe bananas with a fork until smooth, then whisk in the eggs, vanilla extract and milk. Make a well in the centre of the dry ingredients, tip in the wet ingredients and swiftly whisk together to create a smooth, silky batter.

STEP 2

Heat a little knob of butter in a large non-stick pan over a medium heat. Add 2-3 tbsp of the batter to the pan and cook for several minutes, or until small bubbles start appearing on the surface. Flip the pancake over and cook for 1-2 mins on the other side. Repeat with the remaining batter, keeping the pancakes warm in a low oven.

STEP 3

Stack the pancakes on plates and top with the banana slices, a glug of sticky maple syrup and a handful of pecan nuts, if you like.

Easy Singapore noodles

Prep: 15 mins **Cook:** 15 mins

Easy

Serves 4

Ingredients

- 200g vermicelli rice noodles
- 1 tbsp mild curry powder
- ¼ tsp turmeric
- 1 tsp caster sugar
- 1 tbsp sesame oil
- 2½ tbsp low-salt soy sauce
- 1 tbsp sunflower or vegetable oil
- 1 onion , sliced
- 1 pepper , sliced (we used ½ green and ½ orange)
- 200g beansprouts
- 1 red chilli , sliced (optional)

Method

STEP 1

Boil the kettle and put the noodles in a large pan or bowl. Pour over enough boiled water to cover, pushing the noodles under the water to help them soften evenly. Set aside for 5-10 mins, until the noodles are completely soft. Mix the curry powder, turmeric, sugar, sesame oil, soy sauce and 1 tbsp water in a bowl.

STEP 2

Heat the wok until very hot. Add the sunflower oil, onion and pepper. Stir-fry for 3-4 mins until softened and starting to brown in places. Drain the noodles and add to the pan, along with the sauce mixture and beansprouts. Stir-fry for a further 3-4 mins, tossing everything through the sauce, until hot. Adjust the seasoning with a little more soy or sugar, if you like, and scatter over the chilli, if you like more spice.

RECIPE TIPS

THE LOWDOWN ON BEANSPROUTS

Only eat raw beansprouts that are labelled "ready to eat", otherwise cook them thoroughly, and follow the pack storage instructions.

Easy onion bhajis

Prep: 30 mins **Cook:** 20 mins

Easy

Makes 12

Ingredients

- 2 onions, finely sliced
- 100g gram flour
- ½ tsp gluten-free baking powder
- ½ tsp chilli powder
- ½ tsp turmeric
- 1 green chilli, deseeded and very finely chopped
- vegetable oil for frying

For the raita

- ½ cucumber
- 150g tub Greek-style yogurt
- 2 tbsp chopped mint

Method

STEP 1

Soak the onion in cold water while you make the base mix. Sift the flour and baking powder into a bowl, then add the chilli powder, turmeric, chopped chilli and a good sprinkling of salt. Mix in about 100ml of cold water to make a thick batter – add a splash more if it feels too stiff.

STEP 2

For the raita, peel the cucumber and grate it into a sieve set over another bowl. Mix the remaining ingredients with some seasoning and the drained cucumber – squeezing out any extra moisture with your hands – then spoon into a small serving bowl.

STEP 3

Drain the onion well and mix it into the batter. Heat about 5cm of oil in a wok or deep pan. *Do not fill the pan more than a third full.* Add a tiny speck of batter. If it rises to the surface surrounded by bubbles and starts to brown, then the oil is hot enough for frying.

STEP 4

Lower heaped tbsps of the bhaji mixture into the pan, a few at a time, and cook for a few mins, turning once, until they are evenly browned and crisp, so about 3-4 mins. Drain on kitchen paper, sprinkle with a little salt and keep warm while you cook the rest. Serve with the raita.

Easy honey flapjacks

Prep: 8 mins **Cook:** 15 mins

Easy

Makes 12

Ingredients

- 225g butter, plus extra for the tin
- 75g caster sugar
- 4 tbsp honey
- 350g porridge oats

Method

STEP 1

Heat the oven to 180C/160C fan/gas 4. Butter and line a 30 x 15cm rectangle tin with baking parchment. Melt the butter, sugar and honey in a pan over a medium heat, stirring frequently until the butter has melted and the mixture is smooth.

STEP 2

Put the oats in a mixing bowl, then pour over the butter and honey mixture. Stir until all the oats are coated. Tip into the prepared tin, and use a spatula or the back of a spoon to evenly spread out the mixture. Cook for 10-15 mins until lightly golden. Leave to cool in the tin, then remove before cutting into squares.

Easy steak pie

Prep: 15 mins **Cook:** 3 hrs

Easy

Serves 6

Ingredients

- 3 tbsp sunflower oil
- 1kg braising steak, diced
- 2 onions, roughly chopped
- 3 tbsp plain flour
- 1 tbsp tomato ketchup
- 2 beef stock cubes mixed with 600ml boiling water
- 375g sheet of ready-rolled puff pastry
- 1 egg yolk, beaten

Method

STEP 1

To make the filling, heat the oven to 160C/140C fan/gas 3. Heat half the oil in a large casserole dish, brown the meat really well in batches, then set aside. Add the onions adding a drizzle more oil, then cook on a low heat for 5 mins until coloured.

STEP 2

Scatter over the flour, stirring until the flour turns brown. Tip the meat and any juices back into the pan along with the ketchup and give it all a good stir. Pour over the stock, season, and bring to a simmer then cover with a lid and put in the oven for about 2 hrs, until the meat is tender. *The filling can be made up to three days ahead and chilled or frozen for up to three months.*

STEP 3

To make the pie, heat the oven to 220C/200C fan/gas 7. Tip the filling into a 24-26cm rimmed pie dish and brush the rim of the dish with some yolk. Unravel the pastry, drape over the dish and use a knife to trim and press the edges against the side of the dish. Re-roll your trimmings to make a decoration if you like. Brush the pie heavily with egg yolk. Make a few little slits in the centre of the pie and bake for 40 mins until golden. Leave to stand for a few minutes before serving.

Easy chocolate chip cookies

Prep: 20 mins **Cook:** 12 mins

Easy

Makes 10

Ingredients

- 120g butter, softened
- 75g light brown sugar
- 75g golden caster sugar
- 1 medium egg
- 1 tsp vanilla extract
- 180g plain flour
- ½ tsp bicarbonate of soda
- 150g dark chocolate, cut into chunks

Method

STEP 1

Heat oven to 180C/160C fan/gas 4 and line two baking sheets with parchment. Cream the butter and sugars together until very light and fluffy, then beat in the egg and vanilla. Once combined, stir in the flour, bicarb, chocolate and ¼ tsp salt.

STEP 2

Scoop 10 large tbsps of the mixture onto the trays, leaving enough space between each to allow for spreading. Bake for 10-12 mins or until firm at the edges but still soft in the middle – they will harden a little as they cool. Leave to cool on the tray for a few mins before eating warm, or transfer to a wire rack to cool completely. *Will keep for three days in an airtight container.*

Easy banoffee pie

Prep: 25 mins

plus chilling

Easy

Serves 8-10

Ingredients

- 225g digestive biscuits
- 150g butter , melted
- 397g can caramel or 400g dulce de leche
- 3 small bananas , sliced
- 300ml double cream
- 1 tbsp icing sugar
- 1 square dark chocolate (optional)

Method

STEP 1

Crush the digestive biscuits, either by hand using a wooden spoon, or in a food processor, until you get fine crumbs, tip into a bowl. Mix the crushed biscuits with the melted butter until fully combined. Tip the mixture into a 23cm loose bottomed fluted tart tin and cover the tin, including the sides, with the biscuit in an even layer. Push down with the back of a spoon to smooth the surface and chill for 1 hr, or overnight.

STEP 2

Beat the caramel to loosen and spoon it over the bottom of the biscuit base. Spread it out evenly using the back of a spoon or palette knife. Gently push the chopped banana into the top of the caramel until the base is covered. Put in the fridge.

STEP 3

Whip the cream with the icing sugar until billowy and thick. Take the pie out of the fridge and spoon the whipped cream on top of the bananas. Grate the dark chocolate over the cream, if you like, and serve.

Easy beef burritos

Prep: 15 mins **Cook:** 30 mins

Easy

Makes 8/serves 4

Ingredients

- 2 tbsp sunflower oil
- 1 onion, finely chopped
- 4 garlic cloves, very finely chopped
- 1 tbsp ground cumin
- 1 tbsp ground coriander
- small pinch of cayenne pepper (more if you want it spicier)
- 1 tsp dried oregano
- 500g beef mince
- pinch of golden caster sugar
- 1 tbsp wine vinegar or cider vinegar
- 400g can chopped tomatoes
- 400g can black beans or kidney beans, with the can water
- 8 flour or corn tortillas
- 500g cooked rice, or our Mexican tomato rice (see recipe below right)
- a selection of sliced avocado or guacamole, chopped tomatoes, soured cream, shredded lettuce, sliced red onion, grated cheddar, sliced red chilli and lime halves, to serve

Method

STEP 1

Heat the oil in a large pan – a casserole is ideal. Fry the onions for 8 mins, then add the garlic, spices and oregano and cook for 1 min. Crumble over the mince and sizzle for 5 mins, stirring, until browned. Stir in the sugar and leave for a minute, then splash in the vinegar and pour in the tomatoes.

STEP 2

Simmer for 5 mins then tip in the beans and the water from the can. Season, stir and simmer everything for 20 mins until the beef is in a thick gravy. The sauce can be prepared up to 2 days ahead, chilled and reheated with a splash of water or frozen for 6 months.

STEP 3

To make the burritos, heat the tortillas following pack instructions. Pile some rice and beef sauce along each tortilla and scatter over your choice of topping. Fold over the ends and roll up to seal. Secure by wrapping with foil if you want. Eat immediately.

Easy soda bread

Prep: 5 mins **Cook:** 40 mins

Easy

Cuts into 10 slices

Ingredients

- 500g plain wholemeal flour
- 2 tsp sea salt
- 1 tsp bicarbonate of soda
- 1 tbsp finely chopped rosemary (optional)
- 400ml whole milk
- 1 lemon, juiced
- 2 tsp honey

Method

STEP 1

Heat oven to 200C/180C fan/gas 6. Mix together the flour, salt and bicarb in a bowl. And if you'd like rosemary bread, add the chopped rosemary too.

STEP 2

Mix together the milk and lemon juice in a jug, and wait for a minute as it magically turns into buttermilk. Then stir in the honey, and simply pour it into the flour mixture. Stir it with a knife for a minute until the whole thing comes together into a sticky dough.

STEP 3

Tip onto a floured work surface and shape it into a ball.

STEP 4

Put the ball on a floured baking tray and, using a sharp knife, make a deep cross on top.

STEP 5

Put in the oven and bake for 40 mins.

STEP 6

Cool on a wire rack until warm, then slice and serve.

Easy butter chicken

Prep: 15 mins **Cook:** 35 mins

plus at least 1 hr marinating

Easy

Serves 4

Ingredients

- 500g skinless boneless chicken thighs

For the marinade

- 1 lemon, juiced
- 2 tsp ground cumin
- 2 tsp paprika
- 1-2 tsp hot chilli powder
- 200g natural yogurt

For the curry

- 2 tbsp vegetable oil
- 1 large onion, chopped
- 3 garlic cloves, crushed
- 1 green chilli, deseeded and finely chopped (optional)
- thumb-sized piece ginger, grated
- 1 tsp garam masala
- 2 tsp ground fenugreek
- 3 tbsp tomato purée
- 300ml chicken stock
- 50g flaked almonds, toasted

To serve (optional)

- cooked basmati rice
- naan bread
- mango chutney or lime pickle
- fresh coriander
- lime wedges

Method

STEP 1

In a medium bowl, mix all the marinade ingredients with some seasoning. Chop the chicken into bite-sized pieces and toss with the marinade. Cover and chill in the fridge for 1 hr or overnight.

STEP 2

In a large, heavy saucepan, heat the oil. Add the onion, garlic, green chilli, ginger and some seasoning. Fry on a medium heat for 10 mins or until soft.

STEP 3

Add the spices with the tomato purée, cook for a further 2 mins until fragrant, then add the stock and marinated chicken. Cook for 15 mins, then add any remaining marinade left in the bowl. Simmer for 5 mins, then sprinkle with the toasted almonds. Serve with rice, naan bread, chutney, coriander and lime wedges, if you like.

Easy jam tarts

Prep: 25 mins **Cook:** 18 mins

Plus chilling

Easy

Serves 12

Ingredients

- 250g plain flour, plus extra for dusting
- 125g butter, chilled and diced, plus extra for the tin
- 1 medium egg
- 1 vanilla pod, seeds scraped (optional)
- 100g jam, fruit curd or marmalade of your choice

Method

STEP 1

Put the flour, butter and a pinch of salt in a bowl and rub them together with your fingertips (or you can pulse these ingredients together in a food processor if you have one). When the mixture looks and feels like fresh breadcrumbs, stir in the egg and vanilla seeds, if using, with a cutlery knife. Add 1 tbsp cold water, then start to bring the dough together in one lump with your hands – try not to knead it too much. Add 1 more tbsp of water if it's not coming together, but try not to add more than that. Wrap in cling film and chill in the fridge for 30 mins.

STEP 2

Heat oven to 200C/180C fan/gas 6. Butter a 12-hole tart tin, then dust your work surface with flour. Unwrap and roll out the chilled pastry so it's about the thickness of a £1 coin, then use a straight or fluted round cutter to cut out 12 circles, big enough to line the holes in the tin. Dollop 1-2 tsp of your chosen filling into each one and, if you like, cut out little pastry hearts (perfect for Valentine's Day) and pop them on top.

STEP 3

Bake for 15-18 mins or until golden and the filling is starting to bubble a little. Leave to cool in the tin for a few mins then carefully transfer to a wire rack to cool completely.

Easy salad dressing

Prep: 5 mins

No cook

Easy

Serves 4

Ingredients

- 1 tbsp Djion mustard
- 100ml olive oil
- 2 tbsp white wine vinegar
- small pinch sugar

Method

STEP 1

Spoon the mustard into a bowl and slowly whisk in the oil with a small whisk. Gradually add the vinegar and 1 tsp of water to make a creamy looking dressing. Season with the sugar and a generous pinch of salt. *Will keep in a sealed jar for up to a month, but must be whisked again before serving.*

Easy chocolate bark

Prep: 10 mins

plus chilling

Easy

Serves 14

Ingredients

- 200g dark chocolate, chopped
- 2 tbsp chocolate chips
- small handful pretzel pieces
- 2 tbsp honeycomb pieces

Method

STEP 1

Melt the chocolate in short bursts in the microwave, stirring every 20 secs, until smooth. Spoon onto a parchment-lined baking tray and smooth over with a spatula to make a thinnish layer, around 35 x 20cm.

STEP 2

Sprinkle over the chocolate chips along with the pieces of pretzel and honeycomb, then chill until solid. For neat slices, remove the bark from the fridge and leave for a minute to come to room temperature. Use a sharp knife to cut it into shards (if it's fridge cold, the chocolate will snap rather than cut).

Easy egg muffins

Prep: 15 mins **Cook:** 25 mins

Easy

Makes 8 (serves 4)

Ingredients

- 1 tbsp oil
- 150g broccoli, finely chopped
- 1 red pepper, finely chopped
- 2 spring onions, sliced
- 6 large eggs
- 1 tbsp milk
- large pinch of smoked paprika
- 50g cheddar or gruyère, grated
- small handful of chives, chopped (optional)

Method

STEP 1

Heat the oven to 200C/180C fan/gas 4. Brush half the oil in an 8-hole muffin tin. Heat the remaining oil in a frying pan and add the broccoli, pepper and spring onions. Fry for 5 mins. Set aside to cool.

STEP 2

Whisk the eggs with the milk, smoked paprika and half the cheese in a bowl. Add the cooked veg. Pour the egg mixture into the muffin holes and top each with the remaining cheese and a few chives, if you like. Bake for 15-17 mins or until golden brown and cooked through.

Easy gravy

Prep: 5 mins **Cook:** 25 mins

Easy

Serves 6

Ingredients

- 2 tbsp butter
- 2 tbsp plain flour
- 150ml port
- 2 tbsp redcurrant jelly
- 1.6l chicken, turkey or beef stock

Method

STEP 1

Heat the butter in a saucepan (or in a roasting tin containing meat juices from your roast), then scatter over the flour. Stir until it forms a dark, sandy paste. Splash in the port, stir in the redcurrant jelly and cook down until sticky. Stir in the stock and simmer for 5 mins. Decant into a warmed gravy jug to serve.

Easy piccalilli

Prep: 15 mins **Cook:** 10 mins

plus 4 hrs salting and pickling

Easy

Makes 3 x 500ml jars

Ingredients

- 500g cauliflower , cut into small florets
- 200g courgette , cut into small chunks
- 100g green beans or French beans, trimmed and cut into small pieces
- 200g shallots , peeled and cut into small chunks or pearl onions, peeled and left whole or halved
- 600ml malt vinegar
- 3 tbsp English mustard powder
- 1 tbsp coriander seeds
- 2 tbsp black or yellow mustard seeds
- 2 tsp cumin seeds
- 1 tsp turmeric
- 4 tbsp plain flour
- 200g caster sugar
- 2 bay leaves

Method

STEP 1

Put the veg in a bowl and toss with 2 tbsp sea salt. Leave, covered at room temperature, for 4 hrs. Drain the veg and wash well under cold water. Drain well.

STEP 2

Put 100ml of the vinegar in a bowl with the mustard powder, coriander seeds, mustard seeds, cumin, turmeric and flour. Mix well to make a paste.

STEP 3

Heat the remaining 500ml vinegar, sugar, bay leaves and a pinch of salt until the sugar dissolves, then pour in the mustard vinegar mix, simmering and stirring for 5 mins until the mixture thickens. Fold in the drained veg, heat for 1 min taking the edge off the veg, but still retaining a bite, then remove from the heat, and pack into three 500ml warm sterilised jars. *Seal and leave in a cool dark spot for six weeks or up to three months before opening. Once open, keep in the fridge and use within four weeks.*

RECIPE TIPS

HOW TO STERILISE JARS

To sterilise jars, run them through the dishwasher, or wash well in hot soapy water, rinse then dry in a low oven. If you're pickling and recycling old jam jars, it's important to cover the pickle with a wax disk first, so the metal lid doesn't react with the vinegar

Easy beef in black bean sauce

Prep: 15 mins **Cook:** 15 mins

Easy

Serves 4

Ingredients

- 2 x 250g rump steaks
- 1 tbsp cornflour
- 2 tbsp sesame oil
- 1 large white onion, cut into thin wedges
- 1 red pepper, deseeded and sliced
- 1 green pepper, deseeded and sliced
- 2 fat garlic cloves, crushed
- 1 thumb-sized piece ginger, peeled and grated
- 1-2 red chillies, finely chopped

- 5 tbsp black bean sauce
- 1 tbsp rice wine vinegar
- 2 tsp sugar
- sticky rice, to serve
- coriander leaves, to serve (optional)

Method

STEP 1

Remove the thick layer of fat running down the side of the steaks and discard. Slice the steak into 1cm-thick, long strips and toss with the cornflour and some seasoning.

STEP 2

Heat the oil in a large frying pan or wok over a high heat then add the steak, frying for 3-5 mins or until golden brown on the outside. Remove with a slotted spoon and transfer to a plate.

STEP 3

Add the onion and peppers to the pan and fry for 6-7 mins or until beginning to soften. Stir through the garlic, ginger and chilli and cook for a further min. Return the beef to the pan and stir through the black bean sauce, rice wine vinegar, sugar and 2 tbsp water to loosen a little. Bring to a simmer and then remove from the heat.

STEP 4

Serve the stir-fry in deep bowls with mounds of sticky rice and top with coriander, if you like.

Easy green vegetable soup

Prep: 10 mins **Cook:** 15 mins

Easy

Serves 6

Ingredients

- 1 bunch spring onions, chopped
- 1 large potato, peeled and chopped
- 1 garlic clove, crushed
- 1l vegetable stock
- 250g frozen peas
- 100g fresh spinach
- 300ml natural yogurt
- few mint leaves, basil leaves, cress or a mixture, to serve

Method

STEP 1

Put the spring onions, potato and garlic into a large pan. Pour over the vegetable stock and bring to the boil.

STEP 2

Reduce the heat and simmer for 15 mins with a lid on or until the potato is soft enough to mash with the back of a spoon.

STEP 3

Add the peas and bring back up to a simmer. Scoop out around 4 tbsp of the peas and set aside for the garnish.

STEP 4

Stir the spinach and yogurt into the pan, then carefully pour the whole mixture into a blender or use a stick blender to blitz it until it's very smooth. Season to taste with black pepper.

STEP 5

Ladle into bowls, then add some of the reserved cooked peas and scatter over your favourite soft herbs or cress. Serve with crusty bread, if you like.

Easy caponata stew

Prep: 5 mins **Cook:** 15 mins - 20 mins

Easy

Serves 2

Ingredients

- 1 tbsp olive oil, plus a splash
- 1 red onion, finely chopped
- 1 aubergine, cut into 1cm cubes
- 1 garlic clove, peeled
- 1 tsp dried oregano
- 2 tbsp capers
- 400ml can cherry tomatoes
- 2 slices of crusty bread
- ½ small pack of basil
- ½ lemon, juiced

Method

STEP 1

Heat the olive oil in a high-sided frying pan over a high heat, add the onion and aubergine with a big pinch of salt and fry until golden and softened, around 10 mins. Crush in the garlic with the oregano and cook for 1 min max, then tip in the capers and tomatoes. Half fill the empty can with water and add to the pan, bring to the boil then turn the heat down to a simmer until the sauce has thickened and the veg softened.

STEP 2

Toast the bread, then drizzle with a little more olive oil. Squash the cherry tomatoes a bit with the back of a spoon, then stir in half the basil and season the caponata, adding lemon juice, salt and black pepper to taste. Tip into bowls, top with the remaining basil and serve.

Easy chicken burritos

Prep: 10 mins **Cook:** 15 mins

Easy

(makes 6 burritos)

Ingredients

- 1 tbsp vegetable oil
- 1 onion , diced
- 1 tbsp chipotle paste
- 250g cooked chicken , chopped into small chunks
- 2 x 250g pack ready-cooked rice
- 400g can red kidney beans
- 1 lime , juiced
- small bunch coriander , chopped
- 1 ripe avocado , chopped
- 6 large wraps
- 6 tbsp tomato salsa
- 100g grated cheddar
- 6 tbsp soured cream (optional)

Method

STEP 1

Heat the oil in a frying pan and gently fry the onion until soft, about 10 minutes. Stir in the chipotle paste and the chicken to warm through.

STEP 2

Heat the rice following pack instructions and warm through the kidney beans in their liquid in a small pan. Drain the beans and fold in the cooked rice, with half the lime juice and half the coriander.

STEP 3

Mix the remaining coriander and lime juice with the avocado, mashing it well with some seasoning.

STEP 4

Heat the wraps individually in a dry frying pan to warm through, or warm in the microwave for 5-10 seconds.

STEP 5

Divide the rice and beans between the warmed wraps, piling the mixture into the middle of each one. Lay the chicken on top, then add a spoon each of the avocado, salsa, cheddar and soured cream, if using. Don't overfill the wraps or they will be difficult to close.

STEP 6

With each wrap, fold over two ends to cover the filling, then carefully roll over and tuck the ends under to make a thick sausage shape with the folds on the base. Keep the prepared ones warm in a low oven as you work. Cut in half, on a diagonal, to serve.

RECIPE TIPS

CHIPOTLE SUBSTITUTE

If you don't have chipotle paste, mix together 1 tbsp tomato purée, 1 tbsp water, ½ tsp smoked paprika and a pinch chilli flakes.

HOW TO WRAP A BURRITO

If you're having trouble keeping the burritos closed or you're transporting them, use a square of foil underneath each wrap as you're folding it around the filling. Roll tightly, then twist and scrunch the ends. When you're ready to eat, just tear away a strip of foil at one end to keep the filling from falling out of the other.

Easy breakfast burritos

Prep: 40 mins **Cook:** 45 mins

Easy

Serves 8

Ingredients

- 1 tbsp olive oil
- 4 red peppers, finely sliced

For the chipotle baked beans

- 250g chestnut mushrooms, sliced
- 8 spicy or herby sausages

- 1 tbsp olive oil
- 1 red onion, finely chopped
- 400g can pinto beans, drained and rinsed
- 400g can cannellini beans, drained and rinsed
- 400ml passata
- 1-2 tbsp chipotle paste
- 1-2 tbsp red wine vinegar
- 1-2 tbsp light brown soft sugar

For the tomato salsa

- 4 vine tomatoes, finely chopped
- ½ small bunch of coriander, finely chopped
- ½ small red onion, finely chopped
- 1 lime, juiced
- 1 red chilli, deseeded and finely chopped

For the scrambled eggs

- 50g butter
- 1 tsp cumin seeds
- 12 large eggs, beaten

To serve

- 8 large or 16 small tortilla wraps
- 3 large avocados, stoned, peeled and chopped
- ½ small bunch of coriander, roughly chopped
- 50g smoked or mature cheddar, grated
- lime wedges and chilli sauce (optional)

Method

STEP 1

To make the beans, heat the oil in a pan and fry the onion for 5 mins until soft. Add both types of beans, the passata, chipotle paste, vinegar and sugar and simmer for 15 mins until thick and saucy. Season. Add more chipotle paste, sugar or vinegar to taste – it should be a balance of sweet, spicy and tangy. To make the salsa, combine all of the ingredients and season.

STEP 2

Heat the oil in a large frying pan and fry the peppers and mushrooms for 10 mins until soft. Squeeze small chunks of sausagemeat from the sausage skins into the pan and fry for 10 mins more until golden and cooked through.

STEP 3

Warm the tortillas, then keep warm in a clean tea towel. Put the avocados, coriander, cheese and lime wedges (if using) in bowls.

STEP 4

Just before serving, make the scrambled eggs. Heat the butter in a pan and add the cumin seeds. Sizzle for 1 min, then add the eggs, stirring slowly, until scrambled. Season and tip into a warmed bowl. Serve everything in the middle of the table with chilli sauce, if using, and let everyone dig in.

Easy vegan tacos

Prep: 10 mins **Cook:** 30 mins

Easy

Serves 2

Ingredients

- 175g pack baby corn
- 1 large red onion , sliced (190g)
- 1 red pepper , deseeded and roughly chopped
- ½ tsp cumin seeds
- 2 tsp rapeseed oil
- 1 large ripe kiwi , halved lengthways (110g)
- 1 large tomato , halved (115g)
- 100g wholemeal flour , plus extra for rolling
- 1 large garlic clove
- 15g fresh coriander , chopped
- 1 tsp vegan bouillon powder
- ½ tsp smoked paprika
- 85g red cabbage , finely shredded

Method

STEP 1

Heat oven to 220C/200C fan/gas 7. Pile the corn, red onion and pepper into a large shallow roasting tin and toss with the cumin seeds and oil. Add the kiwi and tomato on one side of the tin and roast for 20 mins.

STEP 2

Meanwhile, mix 60ml water into the flour with the blade of a knife to make a dough. Knead briefly until smooth, then cut equally into four and roll out each piece on a lightly floured surface into a 16cm round tortilla. Cover with a tea towel to stop them drying out.

STEP 3

Remove the cooked tomato and kiwi from the tin and return the veg to the oven for 10 mins. Remove the skin from the kiwi and scoop the flesh into a bowl with the tomato, garlic, half the coriander, bouillon and paprika. Use a hand blender to blitz to a smooth salsa.

STEP 4

Heat a large non-stick frying pan, without oil, and cook the tortillas one at a time for a minute on one side and about 10 seconds on the other, until you see them puff up a little. Spread a tortilla with some salsa, top with cabbage and roasted veg, then scatter with the remaining coriander. Add a spoonful more salsa and eat with your hands.

Easy cheesy mustard toad-in-the-hole with broccoli

Prep: 10 mins **Cook:** 40 mins

plus resting

Easy

Serves 4

Ingredients

- 140g plain flour
- 3 large eggs
- 300ml milk
- 2 tsp wholegrain mustard , plus 1 tbsp
- 3 tbsp vegetable oil

For the gravy

- 1 large onion , finely sliced
- 2 tbsp plain flour
- 1 tbsp sherry vinegar

- 6 Cumberland sausages
- 100g long stem broccoli
- 1 leek , cut into thick slices
- 50g mature cheddar , grated

- 3 thyme sprigs
- 600ml fresh chicken stock

Method

STEP 1

Tip the flour and eggs into a large bowl, season and whisk to a thick, smooth paste. Stir in the milk until the batter is the consistency of single cream, then stir in 2 tsp mustard. Leave to rest for 30 mins.

STEP 2

Heat the oven to 240C/220C fan/gas 9. Pour 2 tbsp oil into a heavy roasting tin, casserole dish or ovenproof skillet pan and tip to fully coat with the oil, then put on the middle shelf of the oven for 10 mins. Add the sausages, well spaced apart, and cook for 5-7 mins, then add the broccoli and sliced leek, and cook for another 3 mins. Mash the cheese with the 1 tbsp mustard.

STEP 3

Pour the batter over the sausages, broccoli and leeks, then scatter over most of the mustardy cheese. Cook for 15 mins before turning the oven down to 220C/200C fan/gas 7 (don't open the oven door during this time). Sprinkle over the remaining mustardy cheese, then cook for 5-8 mins until melted, and the batter is puffed and golden brown.

STEP 4

Meanwhile, make the gravy. Fry the onion with the remaining oil for 10-15 mins until lightly golden, adding a little water if they catch. Stir in the flour until it disappears, then add the vinegar and thyme. Season well. Sizzle until the vinegar evaporates, then pour in the stock and bubble uncovered for 10 mins, or until the gravy is the thickness you prefer.

RECIPE TIPS

MAKE IT MEAT FREE

To make a meat-free version, simply use vegetarian sausages and make the gravy with vegetable stock.

Easy vegan pho

Prep: 10 mins **Cook:** 20 mins

Easy

Serves 2

Ingredients

- 100g rice noodles
- 1 tsp Marmite
- 1 tsp vegetable oil

- 50g chestnut mushrooms , sliced
- 1 leek , sliced
- 2 tbsp soy sauce

To serve

- 1 red chilli , sliced (deseeded if you don't like it too hot)
- ½ bunch mint , leaves picked and stalk discarded

- handful salted peanuts
- sriracha , to serve

Method

STEP 1

Tip the noodles into a bowl and cover with boiling water. Leave to stand for 10 mins, then drain, rinse in cold water and set aside.

STEP 2

In a jug, mix the Marmite with 500ml boiling water. Set aside while you cook the vegetables.

STEP 3

Heat the oil in a saucepan, then add the mushrooms and leek. Cook for 10-15 mins until softened and beginning to colour, then add the soy sauce and Marmite and water mixture and stir. Bring to the boil for 5 mins.

STEP 4

Divide the noodles between two deep bowls, then ladle over the hot broth. Top with the chilli slices, mint leaves and peanuts, and serve with some sriracha on the side.

Easy soup maker lentil soup

Prep: 5 mins **Cook:** 30 mins

Easy

Serves 4

Ingredients

- 750ml vegetable or ham stock
- 75g red lentils
- 3 carrots, finely chopped
- 1 medium leek, sliced (150g)
- small handful chopped parsley, to serve

Method

STEP 1

Put the stock, lentils, carrots and leek into a soup maker, and press the 'chunky soup' function. Make sure you don't fill it above the max fill line. The soup will look a little foamy to start, but don't worry – it will disappear once cooked.

STEP 2

Once the cycle is complete, check the lentils are tender, and season well. Scatter over the parsley to serve.

Easy vanilla cupcakes

Prep: 30 mins **Cook:** 15 mins

Plus cooling

Easy

Makes 12

Ingredients

- 110g butter , softened
- 110g golden caster sugar
- 2 eggs
- 1 tsp vanilla extract

For the icing

- 125g butter , softened
- 185g icing sugar

- 110g self-raising flour
- 1-2 tbsp milk , plus a little extra for the icing

Method

STEP 1

Heat oven to 180C/160C fan/gas 4. Line 12 holes in a shallow muffin tin with cupcake cases (not muffin cases). Cream the butter and sugar together until the mixture is light and fluffy. Beat the eggs and vanilla in a jug, then beat into the butter mixture a little at a time.

STEP 2

Fold the flour into the mixture along with a little milk – the mixture should fall easily off a spoon. Divide the mixture between the cases, filling each one no more than half full.

STEP 3

Cook the cakes for 12-15 mins – they should be firm to the touch and slightly golden brown. Cool in the tin for 5 mins, then lift them out gently and leave to cool completely.

STEP 4

To make the icing, beat the butter until it is very soft. Beat in the icing sugar a little at a time, then beat in a splash of the milk as you need to give you a soft icing that can be piped easily. Scrape the icing into an icing bag fitted with a star nozzle. Ice the cakes in swirls, starting in the centre and working outwards.

Easy pound cake

Prep: 10 mins **Cook:** 45 mins

Easy

Serves 8

Ingredients

- 200g unsalted butter, softened
- 200g caster sugar
- 3 eggs, beaten
- 200g self-raising flour
- 1 tsp baking powder
- 3 tbsp whole milk
- 1 tbsp vanilla paste / ½ vanilla pod seeds

For the icing

- 125g icing sugar
- 1 tbsp vanilla paste / ½ vanilla pod seeds

Method

STEP 1

Pre-heat oven to 180C/160C fan/gas 4 and line a 900g loaf tin with parchment paper (mine was 19cm x 9cm x 6cm). Put all of the ingredients except those for the icing into a large bowl and beat together, either using an electric hand whisk or a wooden spoon until smooth and combined. Pour the mix into the loaf tin and spread evenly with the back of spoon. Bake for 40 – 45 mins.

STEP 2

Once out of the oven, leave to cool and make the icing. Combine the icing sugar and vanilla paste with three tbsp of water – you may need more but add it gradually to get a thick icing. Spread it over the top of the cake; it's fine if it drips down the edges. Allow to set and then slice.

Easy pancakes

Prep: 10 mins **Cook:** 20 mins

Plus optional standing

Easy

Makes 6

Ingredients

- 100g plain flour
- 2 large eggs
- 300ml milk
- 1 tbsp sunflower or vegetable oil, plus a little extra for frying
- lemon wedges to serve (optional)
- caster sugar to serve (optional)

Method

STEP 1

Put 100g plain flour, 2 large eggs, 300ml milk, 1 tbsp sunflower or vegetable oil and a pinch of salt into a bowl or large jug, then whisk to a smooth batter.

STEP 2

Set aside for 30 mins to rest if you have time, or start cooking straight away.

STEP 3

Set a medium frying pan or crêpe pan over a medium heat and carefully wipe it with some oiled kitchen paper.

STEP 4

When hot, cook your pancakes for 1 min on each side until golden, keeping them warm in a low oven as you go.

STEP 5

Serve with lemon wedges and caster sugar, or your favourite filling. *Once cold, you can layer the pancakes between baking parchment, then wrap in cling film and freeze for up to 2 months.*

Easy chicken stew

Prep: 10 mins **Cook:** 50 mins

Easy

Serves 4

Ingredients

- 1 tbsp olive oil
- 1 bunch spring onions, sliced, white and green parts separated
- 1 small swede (350g), peeled and chopped into small pieces
- 400g potatoes, peeled and chopped into small pieces

- 8 skinless boneless chicken thighs
- 1 tbsp Dijon mustard
- 500ml chicken stock
- 200g Savoy cabbage or spring cabbage, sliced
- 2 tsp cornflour (optional)
- crusty bread or cheese scones, to serve (optional)

Method

STEP 1

Heat the oil in a large saucepan. Add the white spring onion slices and fry for 1 min to soften. Tip in the swede and potatoes and cook for 2-3 mins more, then add the chicken, mustard and stock. Cover and cook for 35 mins, or until the vegetables are tender and the chicken cooked through.

STEP 2

Add the cabbage and simmer for another 5 mins. If the stew looks too thin, mix the cornflour with 1 tbsp cold water and pour a couple of teaspoonfuls into the pan; let the stew bubble and thicken, then check again. If it's still too thin, add a little more of the cornflour mix and let the stew bubble and thicken some more.

STEP 3

Season to taste, then spoon the stew into deep bowls. Scatter over the green spring onion slices and serve with crusty bread or warm cheese scones, if you like.

Easy-to-scale cheesy fish pie with kale

Prep: 10 mins **Cook:** 45 mins

Easy

Serves 2

Ingredients

- 200g Maris Piper potatoes, cut into chunks
- 1 tbsp butter
- 1 tbsp flour
- 200ml whole milk, plus 1 tbsp
- ½ tsp Dijon mustard
- 100g cheddar, gruyère or emmental, grated
- 200g fish pie mix (we used a mix of salmon, haddock and prawns)
- 50g frozen peas
- 50g shredded kale
- 1 spring onion, finely sliced
- 1 tbsp parmesan, finely grated
- green salad, to serve (optional)

Method

STEP 1

Tip the potatoes into a pan, cover with hot water from the kettle and add a pinch of salt. Simmer for 15-20 mins until tender, then drain and leave to steam-dry.

STEP 2

Meanwhile, warm the butter in a heavy-based pan over a low heat. Add the flour and stir until you have a paste. Gradually whisk in 200ml milk until you have a thick white sauce. Simmer for 3-4 mins, stirring. Season, then stir in the mustard and half the cheese, and continue to stir until the cheese has melted. Fold in the fish, peas and kale, and cook for 8 mins more, or until the kale wilts, the fish is just cooked and the prawns are starting to turn pink.

STEP 3

Heat the grill to medium-high. Mash the potatoes with the spring onion and 1 tbsp milk. Fold in the remaining cheese and season well.

STEP 4

Tip the filling into a heatproof dish and spoon the cheesy mash on top, swirling it with a fork until the filling is completely covered. Sprinkle over the parmesan and grill for 10-15 mins until the pie is golden and bubbling. Serve with a green salad, if you like. *Uncooked pie, well covered in the dish, will keep in the freezer for up to three months.*

RECIPE TIPS

FISH PIE FISHCAKES

Mash together any leftover cold fish pie. Shape into cakes, then dip them in flour, egg and breadcrumbs to coat. Fry until golden and serve.

Easy sausage & courgette pilaf

Prep: 5 mins **Cook:** 15 mins

Easy

Serves 2

Ingredients

- 100g basmati rice
- 1 tsp vegetable oil

- 3 sausages, meat squeezed from the skins
- 1 tsp fennel seeds, black onion seeds or crushed coriander seeds
- 1 courgette, sliced into half-moons
- 100g frozen peas
- 200ml vegetable stock
- ½ small bunch of mint, leaves picked and finely chopped
- ½ small bunch of dill, finely chopped
- 2 tbsp fat-free yogurt

Method

STEP 1

Rinse the rice a couple of times until the water runs clear, then leave to soak. Heat the oil in a medium saucepan with a tight-fitting lid, and fry the sausagemeat for 2-3 mins until crisp and golden. Stir in the seeds and courgette, and fry for another 2 mins over a high heat so the water from the courgette evaporates.

STEP 2

Stir in the drained rice, peas, stock and half the chopped herbs. Bring to a simmer, then reduce the heat to low and cover with a lid. Cook for 10-12 mins until the rice is tender.

STEP 3

Fold most of the remaining herbs into the rice. Serve with a scattering of the remaining herbs on top and the yogurt on the side.

Easy chocolate mousse

Prep: 5 mins **Cook:** 2 mins

Easy

Serves 4

Ingredients

- 150g 70% dark chocolate, plus extra to serve
- 6 egg whites
- 2 tbsp golden caster sugar
- 4 tbsp crème fraîche and grated chocolate, to serve

Method

STEP 1

Melt the chocolate in the microwave in a microwaveable bowl, stirring every 30 seconds until just melted. Whisk the egg whites to soft peaks, scatter in the sugar and whisk again until the mixture forms stiff peaks when you lift the whisk out (around 30 seconds).

STEP 2

Add a big tablespoon of the egg white to the melted chocolate and mix vigorously, working fast so the chocolate doesn't cool and harden. Then fold in the remaining egg whites carefully using a spatula or large metal spoon. Spoon into 4 glasses or ramekins and set in the fridge for 2-3 hours. Serve each with a dollop of crème fraiche and shavings of dark chocolate.

Easy slow cooker chicken casserole

Prep: 10 mins **Cook:** 4 hrs - 8 hrs

Easy

Serves 4

Ingredients

- 1 leek, roughly chopped
- 1 carrot, roughly chopped
- 1 onion, roughly chopped
- 350g new potatoes, roughly chopped
- 6 skinless, boneless chicken thighs, chopped
- 500ml chicken stock
- 4 tbsp vegetable gravy granules

Method

STEP 1

Put the veg and chicken in a slow cooker. Pour the stock over and around the chicken thighs, then mix in the gravy granules to thicken it up (the sauce will be quite thick – use less gravy if you prefer a runnier casserole).

STEP 2

Switch the slow cooker to low and leave to cook for at least 4 hrs, or up to 8 hrs – try putting it on before you go to work, so that it's ready when you get home. Season well, then serve.

Easy moussaka

Prep: 20 mins **Cook:** 45 mins

Easy

Serves 4

Ingredients

- 4 medium-sized potatoes
- 3 tbsp olive oil, plus extra for brushing
- 1 red onion, sliced
- 500g lamb mince
- 2 garlic cloves, crushed
- 1 tsp mixed spice
- 500g carton passata
- 2 aubergines, cut into slices
- 300ml tub crème fraîche
- 140g cheddar, grated

Method

STEP 1

Boil the potatoes whole for 20 mins or just until tender. Drain and allow to cool.

STEP 2

Return the pan to the heat and add 2 tbsp olive oil and the onion. Cook until softened, then add the lamb. Fry the mince for 5 mins or until cooked through and starting to char. Add the garlic and spice, and stir in the passata. Bring to a simmer, then season to taste, take off the heat and set aside until needed.

STEP 3

Heat oven to 220C/200C fan/gas 7. Warm a griddle pan over a high heat and brush a little oil over the aubergines. Grill for 2-3 mins each side or until char lines appear. You may have to do this in 3-4 batches.

STEP 4

Once cool enough to handle, cut the boiled potatoes into thick slices. Put 1 tbsp oil in the base of a deep ovenproof dish and start with a layer of potatoes, then aubergines, a sprinkling of seasoning, then a layer of the lamb mixture. Repeat until all the mixture is used up, ending with a layer of aubergines. Spread the crème fraîche over the top and scatter with the cheese. Put in the oven for 10 mins or until the cheese is golden.

Easy vegan chocolate cake

Prep: 30 mins **Cook:** 25 mins

plus cooling

Easy

Serves 12 - 16

Ingredients

For the cake

- a little dairy-free sunflower spread, for greasing
- 1 large ripe avocado (about 150g)
- 300g light muscovado sugar
- 350g gluten-free plain flour
- 50g good-quality cocoa powder
- 1 tsp bicarbonate of soda
- 2 tsp gluten-free baking powder
- 400ml unsweetened soya milk
- 150ml vegetable oil
- 2 tsp vanilla extract

For the frosting

- 85g ripe avocado flesh, mashed
- 85g dairy-free sunflower spread
- 200g dairy-free chocolate, 70% cocoa, broken into chunks
- 25g cocoa powder
- 125ml unsweetened soya milk
- 200g icing sugar, sifted
- 1 tsp vanilla extract
- gluten-free and vegan sprinkles, to decorate

Method

STEP 1

Heat oven to 160C/140C fan/gas 3. Grease two 20cm sandwich tins with a little dairy-free sunflower spread, then line the bases with baking parchment.

STEP 2

Put 1 large avocado and 300g light muscovado sugar in a food processor and whizz until smooth.

STEP 3

Add 350g gluten-free plain flour, 50g cocoa powder, 1 tsp bicarbonate of soda, 2 tsp gluten-free baking powder, 400ml unsweetened soya milk, 150ml vegetable oil and 2 tsp vanilla extract to the bowl with ½ tsp fine salt and process again to a velvety, liquid batter.

STEP 4

Divide between the tins and bake for 25 mins or until fully risen and a skewer inserted into the middle of the cakes comes out clean.

STEP 5

Cool in the tins for 5 mins, then turn the cakes onto a rack to cool completely.

STEP 6

While you wait, start preparing the frosting. Beat together 85g ripe avocado flesh and 85g dairy-free sunflower spread with electric beaters until creamy and smooth. Pass through a sieve and set aside.

STEP 7

Melt 200g dairy-free chocolate, either over a bowl of water or in the microwave, then let it cool for a few mins.

STEP 8

Sift 25g cocoa powder into a large bowl. Bring 125ml unsweetened soya milk to a simmer, then gradually beat into the cocoa until smooth. Cool for a few mins.

STEP 9

Tip in the avocado mix, 200g sifted icing sugar, melted chocolate and 1 tsp vanilla, and keep mixing to make a shiny, thick frosting. Use this to sandwich and top the cake.

STEP 10

Cover with sprinkles or your own decoration, then leave to set for 10 mins before slicing. *Can be made 2 days ahead.*

RECIPE TIPS

WORKING QUICKLY

You need to spread the frosting quite soon after it's made, as it thickens quickly. If it does thicken, just warm the bowl over a pan of hot water, or give it a few seconds in the microwave, paddling the mixture around with a spatula until it's smooth and shiny.

Easy iced tea

Prep: 5 mins

Plus infusing and chilling

Easy

Serves 6

Ingredients

- 6 tea bags
- 2 tbsp golden caster sugar
- 1 tbsp runny honey, plus extra to serve
- 2 lemons, 1 juiced, 1 sliced
- 1 orange, sliced
- small bunch mint, leaves picked
- ice

Method

STEP 1

Put the tea bags, sugar, honey and 1.5 litres water in a large jug. Leave to infuse for 10 mins, then remove and discard the tea bags. Chill until ready to serve.

STEP 2

Stir in the lemon juice, lemon slices, orange slices and mint leaves. Fill the jug with plenty of ice and stir again.

STEP 3

Fill tall glasses with ice and pour over the iced tea, then serve with extra honey to taste.

RECIPE TIPS

ADJUSTING FLAVOUR

Tea bags can vary in flavour and bitterness, so serving your iced tea with extra honey allows guests to adjust the sweetness to their taste.

Easy classic lasagne

Prep: 15 mins **Cook:** 1 hr

Easy

Serves 4 - 6

Ingredients

- 1 tbsp olive oil
- 2 rashers smoked streaky bacon
- 1 onion , finely chopped
- 1 celery stick, finely chopped
- 1 medium carrot , grated
- 2 garlic cloves , finely chopped
- 500g beef mince
- 1 tbsp tomato purée
- 2 x 400g cans chopped tomatoes
- 1 tbsp clear honey
- 500g pack fresh egg lasagne sheets
- 400ml crème fraîche
- 125g ball mozzarella , roughly torn
- 50g freshly grated parmesan
- large handful basil leaves , torn (optional)

Method

STEP 1

Heat the oil in a large saucepan. Use kitchen scissors to snip the bacon into small pieces, or use a sharp knife to chop it on a chopping board. Add the bacon to the pan and cook for just a few mins until starting to turn golden. Add the onion, celery and carrot, and cook over a medium heat for 5 mins, stirring occasionally, until softened.

STEP 2

Add the garlic and cook for 1 min, then tip in the mince and cook, stirring and breaking it up with a wooden spoon, for about 6 mins until browned all over.

STEP 3

Stir in the tomato purée and cook for 1 min, mixing in well with the beef and vegetables. Tip in the chopped tomatoes. Fill each can half full with water to rinse out any tomatoes left in the can, and add to the pan. Add the honey and season to taste. Simmer for 20 mins.

STEP 4

Heat oven to 200C/180C fan/gas 6. To assemble the lasagne, ladle a little of the ragu sauce into the bottom of the roasting tin or casserole dish, spreading the sauce all over the base. Place 2 sheets of lasagne on top of the sauce overlapping to make it fit, then repeat with more sauce and another layer of pasta. Repeat with a further 2 layers of sauce and pasta, finishing with a layer of pasta.

STEP 5

Put the crème fraîche in a bowl and mix with 2 tbsp water to loosen it and make a smooth pourable sauce. Pour this over the top of the pasta, then top with the mozzarella. Sprinkle Parmesan over the top and bake for 25–30 mins until golden and bubbling. Serve scattered with basil, if you like.

Easy-peasy fruitcake

Prep: 30 mins **Cook:** 3 hrs

Plus soaking

Easy

Serves 14-16

Ingredients

- 4 tbsp rum or brandy
- 1 orange , zested and juiced
- 600g mixed dried fruit (sultanas, raisins, apricots, cherries, cranberries)
- 200g butter , very soft
- 200g golden caster sugar
- 4 eggs
- 50g ground almonds
- 200g plain flour
- 100g pecan nuts or whole skinned almonds, chopped
- 100g candied peel , chopped
- 75g crystallised or candied ginger , chopped

For the decoration

- apricot jam (warmed and sieved) or apricot glaze
- candied pineapple , candied angelica, glacé cherries (a mixture of red, green and yellow if you can find them), crystallised ginger

Method

STEP 1

Put the rum (or brandy), orange zest and juice and mixed dried fruit in a bowl and stir. Leave to soak overnight.

STEP 2

Heat oven to 170C/150C fan/gas 3½. Double line a 20cm tin with baking parchment. Beat the butter and sugar together until light and fluffy. Whisk in the eggs one by one, then fold in the almonds and flour. Add a pinch of salt and fold in the soaked fruit mixture (and any remaining liquid in the bowl), along with the nuts, candied peel and ginger. Spoon the mixture into the tin and level the surface.

STEP 3

Bake for 1 hr, then turn the oven down to 150C/130C fan/gas 2 and bake for a further 2 hrs. Check the cake to see if it's pulling away from the sides of the tin and feels firm on top. If you need to, keep cooking for a further 15 mins. Cool in the tin. If storing in the tin, wrap the cake tightly first. *Will freeze for up to two months.*

STEP 4

To decorate, brush the cake with the apricot jam (or glaze) and arrange your choice of candied fruit on top. *Will keep in a sealed container for up to three weeks.*

Easy sweet & sour chicken

Prep: 5 mins - 10 mins **Cook:** 15 mins

Easy

Serves 4

Ingredients

- 9 tbsp tomato ketchup
- 3 tbsp malt vinegar
- 4 tbsp dark muscovado sugar
- 2 garlic cloves, crushed
- 4 skinless and boneless chicken breast, cut into chunks
- 1 small onion, roughly chopped
- 2 red peppers, seeded and cut into chunks
- 227g can pineapple pieces in juice, drained
- 100g sugar snap peas, roughly sliced
- handful salted, roasted cashew nuts, optional

Method

STEP 1

In a large microwaveable dish, mix the ketchup, vinegar, sugar and garlic thoroughly with the chicken, onion and peppers. Microwave, uncovered, on high for 8-10 mins until the chicken is starting to cook and the sauce is sizzling.

STEP 2

Stir in the pineapple pieces and sugar snap peas and return to the microwave for another 3-5 mins until the chicken is completely cooked. Leave to stand for a few minutes, then stir in the cashews, if using, and serve.

Easy Easter biscuits

Prep: 30 mins **Cook:** 15 mins

plus chilling

Easy

Makes 40

Ingredients

- 250g unsalted butter , softened
- 140g golden caster sugar , plus extra for sprinkling
- 1 medium egg , separated and beaten
- 1 lemon , zested
- generous grating of nutmeg
- 300g plain flour , plus extra for dusting
- ½ tsp fine salt
- 60g currants

Method

STEP 1

Heat the oven to 180C/160 fan/gas 4. Place the butter and sugar in a bowl and beat together with a wooden spoon until well combined. Add the egg yolk, lemon zest and nutmeg and beat again.

STEP 2

Add the flour, salt and currants and mix everything together to make a firm dough, using your hands if necessary. Form into a puck-shape, wrap and chill in the fridge for 30 mins.

STEP 3

Line two large baking sheets with baking parchment and lightly dust your work surface with flour. Cut the dough in half and roll out to a ½ cm thickness. Cut out biscuits using a 6cm fluted cutter, lift onto one of the baking sheets with a palette knife, leaving a little space in between. Repeat with the remaining pastry to make a second tray of biscuits, re-rolling the off-cuts. Chill for 30 mins.

STEP 4

Bake for 7 mins, then remove from the oven, brush with egg white, sprinkle with extra sugar and return to the oven for 7-8 mins or until lightly golden brown. Leave to cool on the trays for 5 mins then carefully transfer to a wire rack to cool completely.

Easy spaghetti Bolognese

Prep: 10 mins **Cook:** 1 hr and 10 mins

Easy

Serves 4

Ingredients

- 3 tbsp olive oil
- 300g beef mince
- 200g pork mince
- 2 large shallots , finely chopped
- 2-3 garlic cloves , crushed
- 500g passata
- 1 tbsp tomato purée
- 100ml red wine
- 1 tsp dried oregano
- 400g spaghetti
- 50g parmesan , finely grated
- a few basil leaves

Method

STEP 1

Put 1 tbsp of the oil in a large saucepan over a medium-high heat, add the beef and fry until well browned. Tip out into a dish and repeat with 1 tbsp oil and the pork. Tip the pork into the dish with the beef and put the pan back on the heat with the remaining oil. Turn the heat down and cook the shallots for 8-10 mins or until very soft, then add the garlic. Tip the meat back into the pan and add the passata, purée, wine and oregano. Stir everything together, cover and simmer over a low heat, stirring occasionally, for 45 mins.

STEP 2

Cook the spaghetti following pack instructions, then stir half the parmesan into the Bolognese. Put a spoonful of the pasta water into the sauce to loosen it if it looks too thick, then drain the spaghetti. For a better flavour, tip the pasta onto the sauce, toss everything together to coat, and season well (or serve with the sauce on top). Add the remaining parmesan and a few basil leaves.

Easy falafels

Prep: 15 mins **Cook:** 20 mins

plus at least 8 hrs soaking

Easy

makes 16

Ingredients

- 250g dried chickpeas or dried split broad beans
- ½ tsp bicarbonate of soda
- 3 garlic cloves
- 1 onion, roughly chopped
- 1 leek, roughly chopped
- 1 celery stick, roughly chopped
- 1 small chilli, roughly chopped (deseeded if you don't like it too hot)
- 1 tsp ground cumin
- 1 tsp cayenne pepper
- 1 tsp sumac
- good handful chopped coriander
- good handful chopped parsley
- 80g gram flour
- 100ml vegetable oil

To serve

- houmous, tabbouleh and pickled red onion & radish (see goes well with), flatbreads, shop-bought or see goes well with (optional)

Method

STEP 1

Soak the chickpeas in cold water for 8 hrs, or overnight.

STEP 2

Drain the chickpeas and pulse with the bicarb in a food processor until roughly chopped. Remove 3/4 of the mixture and set aside.

STEP 3

Add the garlic, vegetables, spices and herbs to the remaining mixture in the processor and purée to a paste. Stir the paste into the rough purée of chickpeas, add the gram flour, season and mix well.

STEP 4

Heat oven to 110C/90C fan/gas 1/4. Heat a large, non-stick frying pan over a medium heat and add some of the oil. Use your hands to form the mixture into patties (there should be enough to make about 16). Fry for 2 mins each side until crisp. Keep in a warm oven while you fry the remainder of the mixture, continuing to add a little oil to the pan with each batch. Serve wrapped in flatbreads, if you like, alongside the houmous, tabbouleh and pickled red onion & radish.

Super-easy birthday cake

Prep: 20 mins **Cook:** 25 mins

Easy

Serves 8

Ingredients

- 225g butter, at room temperature
- 225g golden caster sugar
- 4 large eggs
- 225g self-raising flour
- 3 tbsp whole milk
- 1 tsp vanilla extract
- 2 tbsp cocoa powder

For the pink icing

- 150g butter, very soft
- 300g icing sugar, sifted
- pink food colouring

Method

STEP 1

Heat oven to 180C/160C fan/gas 4. Butter two 18cm loose-based cake tins and line the bases with baking parchment. Beat the butter and sugar in a mixer or by hand, then add the eggs, one at a time, mixing well after each. Fold in the flour, milk and vanilla extract until the mixture is smooth.

STEP 2

Divide the mixture between two bowls. Sift the cocoa powder into one of the bowls. Scrape the vanilla batter into one tin and the chocolate batter into the other and level the tops. Bake for 20-25 mins or until a skewer comes out clean. Cool for 5 mins, then transfer to a wire rack and cool completely.

STEP 3

To make the icing, beat the butter and add the icing sugar a little at a time, beating each lot in until you have a smooth, creamy icing. Add a little pink colour and beat it in (add more if you want a stronger colour). Sandwich the two cakes together with icing and spread the rest on top using a palette knife. Will keep in an airtight container for three days.

Easy huevos rancheros

Prep: 3 mins **Cook:** 7 mins

Easy

Serves 1

Ingredients

- 1 tbsp vegetable oil or sunflower oil
- 1 corn tortilla wrap
- 1 egg
- 200g can black beans, drained
- juice ½ lime
- ½ ripe avocado, peeled and sliced
- 50g feta, crumbled
- hot chilli sauce (we like sriracha)

Method

STEP 1

Heat the oil in a frying pan over a high heat. Add the tortilla and fry for 1-2 mins on each side until crisping at the edges. Transfer to a plate.

STEP 2

Crack the egg into the pan and cook to your liking. Meanwhile, tip the beans into a bowl, season and add a squeeze of lime, then lightly mash with a fork.

STEP 3

Spread the beans over the tortilla, top with the egg, avocado, feta and chilli sauce. Squeeze over a little more lime juice just before eating.

Unbelievably easy mince pies

Prep: 30 mins - 40 mins

Cook: 20 mins

Easy

Makes 18 pies

Ingredients

- 225g cold butter, diced
- 350g plain flour

- 100g golden caster sugar
- 280g mincemeat
- 1 small egg, beaten
- icing sugar, to dust

Method

STEP 1

To make the pastry, rub the butter into the flour, then mix in the golden caster sugar and a pinch of salt.

STEP 2

Combine the pastry into a ball – don't add liquid – and knead it briefly. The dough will be fairly firm, like shortbread dough. You can use the dough immediately, or chill for later.

STEP 3

Heat the oven to 200C/180C fan/gas 6. Line 18 holes of two 12-hole patty tins, by pressing small walnut-sized balls of pastry into each hole.

STEP 4

Spoon the mincemeat into the pies. Take slightly smaller balls of pastry than before and pat them out between your hands to make round lids, big enough to cover the pies.

STEP 5

Top the pies with their lids, pressing the edges gently together to seal – you don't need to seal them with milk or egg as they will stick on their own. *Will keep frozen for up to one month.*

STEP 6

Brush the tops of the pies with the beaten egg. Bake for 20 mins until golden. Leave to cool in the tin for 5 mins, then remove to a wire rack. To serve, lightly dust with the icing sugar. *Will keep for three to four days in an airtight container.*

Strawberry cheesecake in 4 easy steps

Prep: 30 mins

Plus 1 hr and overnight chilling

Easy

Serves 12 - 14

Ingredients

- 250g digestive biscuits
- 100g butter, melted
- 1 vanilla pod

For the topping

- 400g punnet of strawberries, halved
- 25g icing sugar

- 600g full fat soft cheese
- 100g icing sugar
- 284ml pot of double cream

Method

STEP 1

To make the base, butter and line a 23cm loose-bottomed tin with baking parchment. Put the digestive biscuits in a plastic food bag and crush to crumbs using a rolling pin. Transfer the crumbs to a bowl, then pour over the melted butter. Mix thoroughly until the crumbs are completely coated. Tip them into the prepared tin and press firmly down into the base to create an even layer. Chill in the fridge for 1 hr to set firmly.

STEP 2

Slice the vanilla pod in half lengthways, leaving the tip intact, so that the two halves are still joined. Holding onto the tip of the pod, scrape out the seeds using the back of a kitchen knife.

STEP 3

Place the cream cheese, icing sugar and the vanilla seeds in a bowl, then beat with an electric mixer until smooth. Tip in the double cream and continue beating until the mixture is completely combined. Now spoon the cream mixture onto the biscuit base, starting from the edges and working inwards, making sure that there are no air bubbles. Smooth the top of the cheesecake down with the back of a dessert spoon or spatula. Leave to set in the fridge overnight.

STEP 4

Bring the cheesecake to room temperature about 30 mins before serving. To remove it from the tin, place the base on top of a can, then gradually pull the sides of the tin down. Slip the cake onto a serving plate, removing the lining paper and base. Purée half the strawberries in a blender or food processor with the icing sugar and 1 tsp water, then sieve. Pile the remaining strawberries onto the cake, and pour the purée over the top.

RECIPE TIPS

BASE HASN'T SET?

To ensure the base sets properly, the melted butter must be thoroughly mixed through the biscuit crumbs. Make sure you also leave it in the fridge to firm up for at least 1 hr before adding the filling so that the crumbs do not mix into the soft cheese mixture.

FILLING HASN'T SET?

The cheesecake may have needed more time in the fridge. The mixture should be quite firm to begin with, but a long chilling time (preferably overnight) is essential to ensure the filling sets well.

TRY A DIFFERENT FLAVOUR

Lemon: Beat the finely grated zest & juice 2 lemons with the soft cheese & icing sugar instead of the vanilla seeds. Top with lemon curd & leave to chill. **Raspberry:** Replace strawberries with fresh raspberries. **Passion fruit & mango:** Make a delicious sauce by sieving the pulp of 4 passion fruit and sweetening to taste with a little icing sugar. Top the cheesecake with chopped mango, then pour over the sauce, dotting the top with a few of the passion fruit seeds.

CAN'T GET IT OUT OF THE TIN?

If you find the cake difficult to un-mould, either let it sit for a little longer or wipe the outside of the tin with a warm cloth. This heats the edges and should allow you to remove the tin easily.

Easy bibimbap

Prep: 20 mins **Cook:** 15 mins

Easy

Serves 2

Ingredients

- 100g thin beef steak
- 2 tsp light soy sauce, plus extra to serve
- 120g rice
- sunflower oil
- 1 carrot, cut into matchsticks
- 50g spinach

- 2 eggs
- ½ tsp toasted sesame seeds
- thumb sized piece of fresh root ginger, peeled and cut into fine matchsticks

Sauce

- 2 tbsp gochujang or 4 tsp sriracha and 2 tsp white miso paste
- 2 tsp toasted sesame seeds

- 2 tsp cider vinegar
- 4 tsp light soy sauce

Method

STEP 1

Put the steak into a bowl and add the soy sauce.

STEP 2

Boil the rice following packet instructions. Meanwhile heat 1 tsp oil in a frying pan or wok then add the steak, leaving the soy sauce behind in the bowl. Fry quickly at a high temperature until well browned on the outside, put it onto a board and cover with foil to rest. Now fry the carrots in the same pan, stir frying for 2-3 mins until starting to soften then transfer to a plate. Next add the spinach and fry until just wilted (about a minute). Finally fry the eggs, adding a little extra oil if the pan is dry.

STEP 3

When the rice is cooked, drain and pile into 2 bowls. Slice the steak then put it on top of the rice. Next to that add a clump of the cooked carrots, then the spinach and finally the ginger. Scatter the sesame seeds over the top. Stir all of the sauce ingredients together in a bowl and serve alongside the rice. The best way to eat it is to dollop on a good serving of the sauce, break into the egg and stir everything together so the sauce and the runny egg yolk get deliciously mixed up with all the vegetables and steak.

Easy smoked turkey crown

Prep: 10 mins **Cook:** 1 hr and 30 mins

Easy

Serves 4-6

Ingredients

- 1 tbsp smoked paprika
- 1 tsp dried herbs such as rosemary, thyme or oregano
- 2kg turkey crown, on the bone
- 50g soft butter

You will need (optional, if smoking)

- a handful of wood chips (applewood are delicious)

Method

STEP 1

Up to two days ahead, mix the paprika, dried herbs and lots of ground pepper with 1 tbsp flaky sea salt. Season the turkey crown with half of the herby salt mixture, then cover. Mix the remaining herby salt mixture with the butter and chill.

STEP 2

To cook, heat oven to 190C/170C fan/gas 5. Smear the herby butter all over the crown, working it under the skin. Sit the crown on a rack in a large roasting tin, skin-side up, and roast for 1 hr 30 mins, basting with the buttery juices every 30 mins until the skin is crisp and the turkey is cooked all the way through.

STEP 3

Remove the turkey from the oven and set aside. Use a small sheet of foil to make an open package of the wood chips. Place the package in a dry frying pan and heat until smoking, then transfer to the roasting tin. Cover everything in a large tent of foil to trap the smoke and leave the turkey to rest for 20 mins before unwrapping and carving. Save the juices from the tin to make a smoky gravy.

RECIPE TIPS

SMOKING GUN

If you can, try using a smoking gun for an intensely smoky flavour. You can use it – or wood chips – to smoke other things, too, such as a whole roast chicken or a side of cooked trout.

Really easy roasted red pepper sauce

Prep: 10 mins **Cook:** 1 hr

Easy

8 (or 2 meals for 4)

Ingredients

- 4 red peppers (or a mix of red, orange and yellow), cut into chunks
- 2 onions , roughly chopped
- 2 garlic cloves (skin left on)
- 2 tbsp olive oil
- 2 x 400g cans peeled plum tomatoes
- 2 tsp red wine vinegar
- 1 tsp light soft brown sugar

Method

STEP 1

Heat oven to 190C/170C fan/gas 5. Toss the peppers and onions with the garlic and olive oil, and spread out in a roasting tin. Roast for 40 mins, then add the tomatoes, red wine vinegar and sugar, and roast for another 20 mins. Tip into a food processor and blend until smooth. Season to taste.

Easy sausage & fennel risotto

Prep: 15 mins **Cook:** 45 mins

Easy

Serves 4

Ingredients

- 2 tbsp olive oil
- 1 onion , finely chopped
- 1 fennel bulb , finely sliced
- 2 pork sausages
- ½ tsp fennel seeds , crushed
- 2 large garlic cloves , crushed
- 3 thyme sprigs, leaves finely chopped, plus extra to serve
- 400g risotto rice
- 100ml white wine
- 1.4 litres hot chicken stock
- 70g parmesan , finely grated
- 1 lemon , zested and juiced

Method

STEP 1

Heat the oil in a large saucepan, add the onion and fennel and fry for 10 mins or until softened. Raise the heat. Squeeze the sausagemeat out of the skins straight into the pan and fry for 5 mins, or until turning golden brown. Stir through the fennel seeds, garlic and thyme and fry for a further minute.

STEP 2

Tip in the rice and fry for 1 min. Pour the wine into the pan and boil the liquid until reduced by half. Add half the stock and cook until absorbed, stirring constantly. Add the remaining stock, a ladleful at a time, and cook until al dente and not too thick in consistency, stirring constantly for 20-25 mins. Season with black pepper.

STEP 3

Stir through the cheese and lemon, then spoon into four bowls and scatter over the extra thyme leaves to finish.

Easy sangria

Prep: 10 mins

plus at least 1 hr macerating

Easy

Serves 6

Ingredients

- 2 oranges , chopped
- 2 pears , chopped
- 2 lemons , 1 chopped, 1 juiced
- 200g red berries , chopped (we used strawberries and cherries)
- 3 tbsp caster sugar
- 1 tsp cinnamon
- ice
- 750ml bottle light red wine
- 100ml Spanish brandy
- 300ml sparkling water

Method

STEP 1

Put the chopped fruit in a bowl and sprinkle over the sugar and cinnamon, then stir to coat. Cover and leave to macerate in the fridge for at least 1 hr, or ideally overnight.

STEP 2

Fill a large jug with ice. Stir the macerated fruit mixture to ensure the sugar is dissolved, then tip into the jug with the wine and brandy. Stir, then top up with the sparkling water and serve.

Easy slow cooker lamb curry

Prep: 20 mins **Cook:** 8 hrs

Easy

Serves 4

Ingredients

- 650g lamb shoulder, cut into large chunks
- 2 tbsp rapeseed oil
- 2 onions, roughly chopped
- 5 garlic cloves, crushed
- 5cm piece of ginger, grated
- 2 tsp cumin
- 2 tsp garam masala
- 1 tsp cinnamon

- 1 tsp chilli powder (mild or hot)
- 1 green chilli, deseeded if you don't like it hot, chopped
- 1 tbsp tomato purée
- 300g Greek yogurt
- 1 small bunch coriander, chopped
- 2 tbsp toasted flaked almonds
- rice, to serve

Method

STEP 1

Heat the slow cooker if you need to. Season the lamb, then brown it in batches for 5-8 mins using a little oil for each batch. Transfer each batch of lamb to the slow cooker.

STEP 2

Put the onions in a frying pan with a little more oil and fry, stirring, for around 10 mins until tender. Stir in the garlic, ginger, spices, chilli and tomato purée and fry together for 1 min more. Add everything to the slow cooker.

STEP 3

Pour 200ml boiling water into the slow cooker and mix everything well. Cook on a low heat for at least 6 hrs.

STEP 4

After at least 6 hrs of cooking, add the yogurt and stir well. Replace the lid and cook for a further ½ to 1 hrs on low. Don't worry if the sauce splits a little, just stir well before serving. Once cooked, scatter over the coriander and flaked almonds and serve with the rice.

Really easy cinnamon rolls

Prep: 15 mins **Cook:** 15 mins

Easy

Makes 18 small rolls

Ingredients

- 350g can ready-made croissant dough (we used Jus Rol)
- 30g unsalted butter, softened
- 2 tsp cinnamon
- 6 tbsp soft light brown sugar

Method

STEP 1

Heat oven to 180C/160C fan/gas 4. Line a 23cm cake tin with a square of baking parchment so the corners stick up (this will help you to lift the rolls out).

STEP 2

Unroll the croissant dough from the can and lay it out on your work surface. Cut it into three sections along the dotted lines, but don't cut the diagonal line. Spread over a quarter of the butter onto each piece.

STEP 3

Mix the cinnamon and sugar together. Using one square of dough at a time, sprinkle over 2-3 tsp of the sugar and roll up the dough. When you have three rolls, cut each one in half and then each half into three. Arrange the rolls in the tin in two circles – you need to spread them well apart as they will rise and spread. Stick the end bits in among fatter pieces from the centre of the rolls so they cook evenly. Bake for 15 mins or until the rolls are risen and cooked through.

STEP 4

Meanwhile, heat the remaining sugar mix with the remaining butter until you have a thick caramel (don't worry if some of the butter separates out, it will soak into the dough). When the rolls are cooked, pour over the caramel. Leave to cool a little, then eat warm.

Family meals: Easy fish pie recipe

Prep: 15 mins **Cook:** 45 mins

Easy

Serves a family of 4-6 or makes 6-8 toddler meals

Ingredients

- 1kg Maris Piper potatoes, peeled and halved
- 400ml milk, plus a splash
- 25g butter, plus a knob
- 25g plain flour
- 4 spring onions, finely sliced
- 1 x pack fish pie mix (cod, salmon, smoked haddock etc, weight around 320g-400g depending on pack size)
- 1 tsp Dijon or English mustard
- ½ a 25g pack or a small bunch chives, finely snipped
- handful frozen sweetcorn
- handful frozen petits pois
- handful grated cheddar

Method

STEP 1

Heat the oven to 200C/fan 180C/gas mark 6.

STEP 2

Put 1kg potatoes, peeled and halved, in a saucepan and pour over enough water to cover them. Bring to the boil and then simmer until tender.

STEP 3

When cooked, drain thoroughly and mash with a splash of milk and a knob of butter. Season with ground black pepper.

STEP 4

Put 25g butter, 25g plain flour and 4 finely sliced spring onions in another pan and heat gently until the butter has melted, stirring regularly. Cook for 1-2 mins.

STEP 5

Gradually whisk in 400ml milk using a balloon whisk if you have one. Bring to the boil, stirring to avoid any lumps and sticking at the bottom of the pan. Cook for 3-4 mins until thickened.

STEP 6

Take off the heat and stir in 320g-400g mixed fish, 1 tsp Dijon or English mustard, a small bunch of finely snipped chives, handful of sweetcorn and handful of petits pois. Spoon into an ovenproof dish or 6-8 ramekins.

STEP 7

Spoon the potato on top and sprinkle with a handful of grated cheddar cheese.

STEP 8

Pop in the oven for 20-25 mins or until golden and bubbling at the edges. Alternatively, cover and freeze the pie or mini pies for another time.

Super-easy sausage casserole

Prep: 5 mins **Cook:** 50 mins

Easy

Serves 4

Ingredients

- 3 tbsp vegetable, olive or rapeseed oil
- 8 sausages
- 500g bag frozen mixed Mediterranean veg
- 2 x 400g cartons tomatoes with garlic and onions
- 2 x 400g cans butter beans , drained
- 2 thick slices good, crusty bread

Method

STEP 1

Heat oven to 200C/180C fan/gas 6. Heat 2 tbsp oil in a flameproof casserole dish with a lid. Add the sausages and brown until golden all over, then transfer to a plate.

STEP 2

Put the frozen veg in the pan and cook for a few mins to thaw. Add the tomatoes, then half-fill one of the cans with water and pour into the dish. Add the beans, season well and bring the mixture to a simmer. Place the sausages on top of the veg, cover with a lid and cook in the oven for 40 mins.

STEP 3

Heat 1 tbsp oil in a frying pan. Tear the bread into small chunks or coarsley grate it, making chunky crumbs. Fry in the hot oil until crisp. Serve the casserole in bowls and top with the breadcrumbs.

Easy pulled beef ragu

Prep: 20 mins **Cook:** 4 hrs

Easy

8 (or 2 meals for 4)

Ingredients

- 2 tbsp olive oil
- 1kg boneless beef brisket
- 2 onions , finely chopped
- 4 garlic cloves , finely chopped

- 5 carrots, thickly sliced
- 250ml red wine
- 2 x 400g cans chopped tomatoes
- 2 tbsp tomato purée
- 4 bay leaves
- 450g large pasta shapes (such as paccheri, rigate or rigatoni)
- large handful basil leaves, to serve
- grated parmesan, to serve

Method

STEP 1

Heat oven to 150C/130C fan/gas 2. Heat 1 tbsp oil in a flameproof casserole dish and brown the beef all over. Take the beef out of the dish, add the remaining oil and gently cook the onions and garlic for 10 mins until softened.

STEP 2

Add the browned beef back to the dish with the carrots, red wine, tomatoes, tomato purée and bay leaves. Cover with foil and a lid, and slowly cook for 3 - 3 1/2 hrs or until the meat falls apart. Check on it a couple of times, turning the beef over and giving it a good stir to make sure it's coated in the sauce.

STEP 3

Cook the pasta following pack instructions, then drain. Shred the beef – it should just fall apart when you touch it with a fork – then spoon the beef and tomato sauce over the pasta. Scatter with basil and Parmesan before serving.

Easy soup maker roast chicken soup

Prep: 5 mins **Cook:** 30 mins

Easy

Serves 2

Ingredients

- 1 onion, chopped
- 1 large carrot, chopped
- ½ tbsp thyme leaves, roughly chopped
- 700ml chicken stock
- 100g frozen peas
- 150g leftover roast chicken, shredded and skin removed
- 1½ tbsp Greek yogurt
- ½ small garlic clove, crushed
- squeeze lemon juice
- 1 onion, chopped
- 1 large carrot, chopped
- ½ tbsp thyme leaves, roughly chopped
- 700ml chicken stock

- 100g frozen peas
- 150g leftover roast chicken, shredded and skin removed
- 1½ tbsp Greek yogurt
- ½ small garlic clove, crushed
- squeeze lemon juice

Method

STEP 1

Put the onion, carrot, thyme, stock, and peas into a soup maker, and press the 'chunky soup' function. Make sure you don't fill the soup maker above the max fill line.

STEP 2

Once the cycle is complete, stir in the shredded roast chicken, and leave to warm through while you mix the yogurt, garlic and lemon juice together. Season the soup, and pour into bowls. Stir in some of the yogurt and serve.

STEP 3

Put the onion, carrot, thyme, stock, and peas into a soup maker, and press the 'chunky soup' function. Make sure you don't fill the soup maker above the max fill line.

STEP 4

Once the cycle is complete, stir in the shredded roast chicken, and leave to warm through while you mix the yogurt, garlic and lemon juice together. Season the soup, and pour into bowls. Stir in some of the yogurt and serve.

Easy salmon coulibiac

Prep: 20 mins **Cook:** 50 mins

Easy

Serves 6

Ingredients

- 2 eggs
- 3 tbsp olive oil or rapeseed oil
- 200g mushrooms, chopped
- 200g packet cooked brown rice
- ½ small pack dill
- 2 lemons, 1 zested and juiced, 1 cut into wedges, to serve
- 2 tbsp capers, chopped
- 270g packet filo pastry (7 sheets)
- salad leaves, to serve
- 600g salmon fillet, boned and skinned

Method

STEP 1

Boil the eggs for 7 mins, then plunge into cold water. Heat 1 tbsp oil in a frying pan, add the mushrooms and a pinch of seasoning and cook, stirring occasionally, for 8-10 mins until golden. Add the rice, dill, lemon zest and juice, capers and some more seasoning, then remove from the heat.

STEP 2

Line a baking sheet with parchment. Put two sheets of pastry next to each other on the tray, slightly overlapping in the middle. Brush with some oil and top with another two sheets, then repeat with two more sheets. Butterfly the salmon by cutting through the side, but not all the way through, so you can open it like a book. Heat oven to 180C/160C fan/gas 4.

STEP 3

Place the salmon on the pastry and stuff with the rice mixture. Peel and slice the boiled eggs and arrange on the rice. Close up the salmon fillet, season and wrap with the pastry to form a parcel. Scrunch the remaining pastry sheet over the top, drizzle with a little more oil and bake for 40 mins. Serve with lemon wedges and dressed salad leaves.

Easy lamb hotpot

Prep: 15 mins **Cook:** 55 mins

Easy

Serves 3

Ingredients

- 700g large potatoes , peeled
- 1 tbsp sunflower oil , plus extra for brushing
- 1 large white onion , sliced
- 4 carrots , chopped into small pieces
- 12 lamb meatballs
- 450ml chicken gravy (leftover or bought)
- 2 bay leaves
- 2 thyme sprigs

Method

STEP 1

Boil the potatoes in a saucepan of boiling water for 15 mins until par-boiled, then drain and leave to steam dry and cool.

STEP 2

Heat oven to 200C/180C fan/gas 6. Heat the oil in a large frying pan and fry the onion for 10 mins or until starting to soften. Add the carrot and cook for 5 mins until tender. Tip the carrot and onion mixture into a large 2-litre ovenproof dish. Put the pan back over high heat. Fry the lamb meatballs, turning, until golden on the outside. Put the meatballs into the ovenproof dish. Pour over the gravy and tuck in the bay leaves and thyme sprigs.

STEP 3

Thinly slice the cooled potatoes and arrange over the top of the meatballs. Brush the potato with 1-2 tsp oil and add a good grinding of black pepper. Bake in the oven for 20-25 mins until the potatoes are tender and starting to become crisp at the edges, and the gravy is bubbling.

Easy chicken & chickpea tagine

Prep: 10 mins **Cook:** 1 hr and 15 mins

plus chilling

Easy

Serves 4

Ingredients

- 800g skinless boneless chicken thighs , cut into large chunks
- 1 tbsp harissa
- 1 tbsp vegetable oil
- 1 large onion , finely sliced
- 1 tsp ground cinnamon
- 1 tsp ground cumin
- 1 tsp ground turmeric
- 500ml chicken stock
- 400g can chopped tomatoes
- 100g raisins
- 400g can chickpeas , drained and rinsed
- 250g couscous , to serve
- small handful mint , leaves only, to serve

Method

STEP 1

Mix the chicken thighs with the harissa in a large bowl and chill, covered, for 20-30 mins.

STEP 2

Heat the oil in a large flameproof casserole or tagine dish and fry the chicken for 2-3 mins until browned. Remove from the dish and set aside.

STEP 3

Fry the onion for 8-10 mins until soft, then stir in the spices. Return the chicken to the dish, together with the stock, tomatoes and raisins. Season, bring to the boil, then reduce the heat to low. Simmer, covered, for 45 mins.

STEP 4

Add the chickpeas to the dish, and simmer, uncovered, for 15 mins until the sauce reduces slightly and thickens. Serve with couscous and a handful of mint leaves on top.

Easy pesto lasagne

Prep: 10 mins **Cook:** 45 mins

Easy

Serves 4 - 6

Ingredients

- 190g jar pesto
- 500g tub mascarpone
- 200g bag spinach , roughly chopped
- 250g frozen pea
- small pack basil , leaves chopped, and a few leaves reserved to finish
- small pack mint , leaves chopped
- 12 fresh lasagne sheets
- splash of milk
- 85g parmesan , grated (or vegetarian alternative)
- 50g pine nuts
- green salad , to serve (optional)

Method

STEP 1

Heat oven to 180C/160C fan/gas 4. Place the pesto, half the mascarpone and 250ml water (or vegetable stock if you have some) in a pan. Heat and mix until smooth and bubbling. Add the spinach and peas and cook for a few more mins until the spinach has wilted and the peas thawed. Add the herbs and season.

STEP 2

Place a third of the pesto mixture into a baking dish roughly 18 x 25cm. Top with 4 lasagne sheets, then repeat with 2 more layers of sauce and lasagne sheets, finishing with a layer of pasta. Mix enough milk into the remaining mascarpone to make a white sauce consistency, season, then pour over the top. Sprinkle with the Parmesan and pine nuts. Bake for 35-40 mins until golden brown on top and bubbling around the edges. Scatter over the reserved basil leaves and serve with a green salad, if you like.

Easy meatloaf with spaghetti & tomato sauce

Prep: 15 mins **Cook:** 50 mins

Easy

Serves 6

Ingredients

- 2 tbsp olive oil , plus extra for greasing and drizzling
- 2 onions , finely chopped
- 500g pork mince
- 1 large egg
- 75g fresh breadcrumbs
- 15 sage leaves , roughly chopped
- 100g feta , crumbled
- 3 bay leaves , 1 finely chopped
- 680g jar passata
- 600g spaghetti

Method

STEP 1

Heat oven to 180C/160 fan/gas 4 and grease an ovenproof dish. Heat the oil in a large frying pan over a medium heat, add the onions, sizzle for 5 mins, then remove half and put in a large bowl with the mince, egg, breadcrumbs, sage, feta and chopped bay. Season well and mix. Shape into a long sausage shape and transfer to the greased dish. Put the remaining bay leaves on top, drizzle with a little more oil and put in the oven for 40-45 mins until cooked through.

STEP 2

Meanwhile, keep the remaining onions on a low heat in the pan. Cook for 2 mins, then increase the heat and pour in the passata with 70ml water. Bubble for 30 mins on a low heat, stirring often, or until the meatloaf is ready to come out of the oven. Season to taste.

STEP 3

Cook the spaghetti following pack instructions. When everything is ready, toss the spaghetti in the tomato sauce, slice the meatloaf and let everyone help themselves.

Quick & easy tiramisu

Prep: 15 mins

plus 1 hr chilling, No cook

Easy

Serves 2

Ingredients

- 3 tsp instant coffee granules
- 3 tbsp coffee liqueur (or Camp Chicory & Coffee Essence)
- 250g tub mascarpone
- 85g condensed milk
- 1 tsp vanilla extract
- 4-6 sponge fingers
- 1 tbsp cocoa powder

Method

STEP 1

Mix the coffee granules with 2 tbsp boiling water in a large jug and stir to combine. Add the coffee liqueur and 75ml cold water. Pour into a shallow dish and set aside.

STEP 2

Make the cream layer by beating the mascarpone, condensed milk and vanilla extract with an electric whisk until thick and smooth.

STEP 3

Break the sponge fingers into two or three pieces and soak in the coffee mixture for a few secs. Put a few bits of the sponge in the bottom of two wine or sundae glasses and top with the cream. Sift over the cocoa and chill for at least 1 hr before serving.

RECIPE TIPS

USES FOR SPONGE FINGERS

Sponge fingers make an ideal base for trifles too. Use leftovers in a super-quick version: pour a little syrup from any canned fruit over the fingers to soak them, then top with cream and the fruit from the can.

STORING LEFTOVER CONDENSED MILK

Once opened, the remaining condensed milk can be stored in an airtight container in a cool, dry place for up to three months.

Easy sourdough bread

Prep: 30 mins **Cook:** 25 mins - 30 mins

plus overnight fermenting and rising

More effort

Makes 1 loaf (cuts into 10-12 slices)

Ingredients

For the starter

- 100g strong white bread flour
- 100g organic dark rye flour
- 0.5 x 7g sachet fast-action dried yeast

For the main dough

- 400g strong white bread flour
- 0.5 x 7g sachet fast-action dried yeast

Method

STEP 1

To make your starter, place all the ingredients in a bowl and add 250ml cold water. Mix together thoroughly with a spoon until you have a spongy mixture, then cover with cling film and leave at room temperature at least overnight, but up to 24 hrs if you have time.

STEP 2

To make the bread dough, tip the ingredients into a clean bowl and add 1 tbsp fine salt, 200ml cold water and your starter. Bring all the ingredients together to a dough, adding a splash more water if too stiff, then tip out onto a lightly floured surface and knead for at least 10 mins until smooth, elastic and springy (this will take 5-7 mins in a mixer with a dough hook). Place the dough in a clean, lightly oiled bowl, cover with cling film and leave until doubled in size – about 1 hr at room temperature, 3 hrs in the fridge (see tips, below).

STEP 3

Tip the dough onto a floured surface and gently shape into a round – you don't want to knock too much air out of the dough. Dust a piece of baking parchment heavily with flour and sit the dough on top. Cover with a tea towel and leave to prove for 1 hr until doubled in size.

STEP 4

Heat oven to 220C/200C fan/gas 7. Place a sturdy flat baking tray on the middle shelf of the oven and a smaller tray with sides underneath. Dust the dough with flour and slash with a utility knife. Slide the bread onto the hot tray on top and throw a few ice cubes (or pour some cold water) onto the tray below – this creates a burst of steam, which helps the bread form a nice crust. Bake for 25-30 mins until the loaf sounds hollow when tapped on the bottom. Leave the bread to cool completely.

RECIPE TIPS

DEVELOP THE FLAVOUR

The longer it takes a bread dough to rise, the more flavour it develops. For the best flavour and the slowest rise, leave the dough in the fridge – the cool temperature means that it will take longer for the yeast to work.

FOR REGULAR BAKERS

If you want to make this bread on a regular basis, keep back about 100ml of the starter and a small handful of the kneaded dough. Put the two together in a jar, keep it in the fridge and use as the base to your next starter and loaf. Repeat every time you make a loaf. The pre-fermented base to a new starter will give it even more of a sourdough flavour.

Easy falafel burgers

Prep: 10 mins **Cook:** 10 mins

Easy

Serves 4

Ingredients

- 250g chickpeas from a can
- 1 medium onion, finely chopped
- 2 garlic cloves, crushed
- 2 tsp ground coriander
- 2 tsp ground cumin
- small pack flat-leaf parsley, chopped
- 2 rounded tbsp plain flour
- 2 tbsp vegetable oil
- 100g hummus
- 4 burger buns, cut in half
- watercress, to serve

Method

STEP 1

Drain, rinse and dry the chickpeas thoroughly, then tip into the bowl of a food processor. Pulse until lightly broken up into coarse crumbs.

STEP 2

Add the onion, garlic, spices, parsley, flour and some seasoning, and continue to pulse until combined. Using your hands, gently form the mixture into 4 patties about 10cm in diameter and 2cm thick.

STEP 3

In a large pan, heat the oil and fry the falafels on each side for 2-3 mins or until golden (you may need to do this in batches). Lightly griddle the burger buns on the cut side in a griddle pan, or toast under the grill.

STEP 4

Spread one side of each bun with hummus, top with a falafel burger, add a handful of watercress, then pop the remaining bun half on top.

Easy lentil pastries

Prep: 20 mins **Cook:** 20 mins

Easy

Makes 24 (serves 6 as a starter)

Ingredients

- 320g shortcrust pastry sheet
- 250g pouch French tomatoey green & Puy lentils (we used Merchant Gourmet)
- 100g feta
- 1 egg

Method

STEP 1

Heat oven to 200C/180C fan/gas 6. Unroll the pastry and cut into 24 squares. Divide the lentils and feta between the pastry squares, leaving a border around the edge. Beat the egg and brush a little of it onto the edges of the pastry, then pinch together to seal in a cross shape at the top. Transfer the pastries to a large baking sheet, brush with the remaining beaten egg and bake for 20 mins until golden. Serve as a starter with dressed leaves.

Easy flatbread

Prep: 10 mins **Cook:** 10 mins

Easy

Makes 8

Ingredients

- 400g gluten-free self-raising flour, plus extra for dusting (we used Doves)
- 1 tbsp cumin seeds, toasted
- 300ml natural yogurt

Method

STEP 1

Heat the grill to medium and dust a baking sheet with a little flour. Mix the flour and cumin seeds in a bowl, then season. Stir in the yogurt and 100ml water, then mix well to form a soft dough.

STEP 2

Divide the dough into 8 equal pieces, then shape into circles or ovals about ½cm thick. Dust lightly with a little flour. Grill on the baking sheet for 3-5 mins on each side until golden and puffed. Serve warm.

Easy turkey crown

Prep: 10 mins **Cook:** 1 hr and 30 mins

Easy

Serves 4 - 6

Ingredients

- 50g butter, softened
- 2kg turkey crown on the bone
- 1 tsp Chinese five spice or a pinch of ground cloves

For the glaze

- 4 tbsp honey
- 1 tbsp Dijon mustard
- 1 tbsp red wine vinegar

Method

STEP 1

Heat oven to 190C/170C fan/gas 5. Smear the butter all over the turkey crown and season all over with salt and half the five spice. Put in a roasting tin, skin-side up, and roast for 30 mins. While the crown is roasting, mix all the glaze ingredients in a bowl with the rest of the five spice.

STEP 2

Remove the crown from the oven and brush the skin generously with half the glaze. Continue to roast for another hour, glazing twice more, until cooked all the way through and the glaze is sticky and caramelised. Leave to rest for at least 20 mins before carving. Save the juices from the tin to make gravy.

Easy creamy coleslaw

Prep: 20 mins

No cook

Easy

Serves 4

Ingredients

- ½ white cabbage, shredded
- 2 carrots, grated
- 4 spring onions, chopped
- 2 tbsp sultanas
- 3 tbsp low-fat mayonnaise
- 1 tbsp wholegrain mustard

Method

STEP 1

Put the cabbage, carrots, spring onions and sultanas in a large bowl and stir to combine.

STEP 2

Mix the mayonnaise with the mustard in another small bowl and drizzle over the veg. Fold everything together to coat in the creamy sauce, then season to taste.

Easy creamed spinach

Prep: 2 mins **Cook:** 6 mins

Easy

Serves 2

Ingredients

- 1 tbsp butter
- 200g spinach
- 75ml double cream
- 3 tbsp grated parmesan (or vegetarian alternative)
- grating of nutmeg (optional)

Method

STEP 1

In a large sauté pan, heat the butter over a medium heat. Tip in the spinach and wilt for 5 mins until all the liquid from the spinach has evaporated.

STEP 2

Add the double cream and grated Parmesan. Season well and add a little nutmeg, if you like. Serve as a delicious side to smoked haddock.

Easy fruitcake

Prep: 20 mins **Cook:** 25 mins

Easy

Serves 8

Ingredients

- 175ml flavourless oil, plus extra for greasing
- 100g light brown muscovado sugar
- 2 eggs, beaten
- 225g plain flour
- 1 tsp baking powder
- 1 tsp ground cinnamon
- ½ tsp allspice
- ½ orange, juiced
- ½ lemon, juiced
- 200g mixed dried fruit
- 200g apricot jam
- icing sugar, for dusting

Method

STEP 1

Heat oven to 160C/140C fan/ gas 3. Grease and line the base of two 20cm springform cake tins with baking parchment.

STEP 2

Stir together the oil and sugar, add the eggs, flour, baking powder, spices and juices, and mix thoroughly with a wooden spoon until pourable and reasonably runny. Gently fold in the fruit, then divide the batter evenly between the tins. Bake for 20-25 mins or until a skewer inserted in the centre comes out clean, then leave to cool.

STEP 3

When cool, remove from the tins and sandwich the cakes together with jam. Sieve some icing sugar on top to serve.

Easy risotto with bacon & peas

Prep: 5 mins **Cook:** 40 mins

Easy

Serves 4

Ingredients

- 1 onion
- 2 tbsp olive oil
- knob of butter
- 6 rashers streaky bacon, chopped
- 300g risotto rice
- 1l hot vegetable stock
- 100g frozen peas
- freshly grated parmesan, to serve

Method

STEP 1

Finely chop 1 onion. Heat 2 tbsp olive oil and a knob of butter in a pan, add the onions and fry until lightly browned (about 7 minutes).

STEP 2

Add 6 chopped rashers streaky bacon and fry for a further 5 minutes, until it starts to crisp.

STEP 3

Add 300g risotto rice and 1l hot vegetable stock, and bring to the boil. Stir well, then reduce the heat and cook, covered, for 15-20 minutes until the rice is almost tender.

STEP 4

Stir in 100g frozen peas, add a little salt and pepper and cook for a further 3 minutes, until the peas are cooked.

STEP 5

Serve sprinkled with freshly grated parmesan and freshly ground black pepper.

Easy mackerel bowls

Prep: 20 mins **Cook:** 15 mins

Easy

Serves 4

Ingredients

- 200ml sake
- 60ml mirin
- 3 tbsp white miso
- 3 tbsp palm sugar
- 60ml dark soy sauce
- thumb-sized piece ginger , peeled and sliced into matchsticks
- 4 skinless mackerel fillets, bones removed, cut into thick slices
- 2 x 250g pouches mixed grains
- 80g frozen petits pois
- 1 large courgette , sliced into ribbons with a peeler
- 50g watercress
- 1 tbsp sesame seeds , to serve

Method

STEP 1

Put the sake, mirin, miso, palm sugar and soy in a saucepan and bring to the boil. Add the ginger and return to the boil.

STEP 2

Place the mackerel in a single layer in the saucepan, cover and reduce to a simmer. Cook on a low heat for 5-10 mins, then remove the mackerel and ginger, and taste the broth. If it's a bit strong, dilute with 50-100ml water.

STEP 3

Cook the grains following pack instructions. Tip the peas into a bowl, cover with boiling water, allow to sit for 30 secs, then drain. Spoon the grains into four deep bowls, then spoon about 2 tbsp of the broth into each (you'll have some left over). Top with the mackerel and ginger, a handful of watercress, the peas, courgette and a scattering of sesame seeds.

Easy brownies

Total time 1 hr and 15 mins

Ready in 1 hour 15 minutes, plus cooling time

Easy

Makes 24

Ingredients

- 375g good quality dark chocolate
- 375g butter, cut into pieces
- 500g caster sugar
- 6 medium eggs
- 225g plain flour

For the topping (optional)

- 140g good quality dark chocolate
- 50g butter, cut into pieces
- icing sugar for dusting

Method

STEP 1

Butter and line a 30cm x 21cm tin. Preheat the oven to 180C/160C fan/gas 4. Break up the chocolate with the butter and melt in the microwave on medium for about 5 minutes, stirring halfway through.

STEP 2

Beat the sugar and eggs in a bowl. Stir in the melted chocolate, add the flour and beat well. Pour into the tin and bake for 40-45 minutes, or until the top looks papery and feels slightly wobbly. Leave to cool in the tin.

STEP 3

If you're making the topping, break up the chocolate with the butter and melt in the microwave on medium for about 1 minute. Stir until smooth then spread over the cake. Dust with icing sugar and cut into squares.

Easy yogurt flatbreads

Prep: 20 mins **Cook:** 5 mins

plus 1hr rising

More effort

makes 12

Ingredients

- 500g plain flour
- 1 tsp salt
- 1 tsp golden caster sugar
- 1 tsp fresh yeast or 1/3 tsp fast-action dried yeast
- 150ml full-fat milk
- 150g pot natural yogurt
- 60g clarified butter or ghee

Method

STEP 1

Put the flour, salt, sugar and yeast in a large bowl and mix well. Heat the milk in a saucepan until lukewarm. Reserving 1 tbsp of the yogurt, add the rest to the milk and mix thoroughly. Melt the butter and add to the milk and yogurt, mixing well.

STEP 2

Pour slowly over the flour and mix together, then knead for 10 mins until you have a springy dough. Leave to rise in a warm place for about 1 hr until doubled in size.

STEP 3

Divide the dough into 10 even- sized balls. Heat the grill to medium and put a large baking tray under it to heat for about 10 mins. Flatten the balls of dough, roll into rough teardrop shapes and spread with the reserved yogurt. Place on the hot baking tray and grill under a moderate heat for 2-3 mins each side until golden. Watch constantly, as they can burn very quickly.

Easy hummus recipe

Prep: 5 mins

No cook

Easy

Makes 4 snack portions

Ingredients

- 1 x 400g can chickpea , don't drain
- 1 tbsp tahini paste
- 1 fat garlic clove , chopped
- 3 tbsp 0% fat Greek yogurt
- good squeeze lemon juice

Method

STEP 1

Drain the chickpeas into a sieve set over a bowl or jug to catch the liquid. Tip the chickpeas, tahini, garlic and yogurt into a food processor or blender and whizz to smooth.

STEP 2

Whizz in a tbsp of the chickpea liquid at a time until you have a nice consistency, then scrape into a bowl.

STEP 3

Stir in a squeeze of lemon juice and season to taste.

Easy cherry jam

Prep: 25 mins **Cook:** 50 mins

Easy

Makes 4 x 150g jars

Ingredients

- 2kg cherries , pitted, ½ roughly chopped, ½ halved
- 1.2kg jam or preserving sugar (with added pectin)
- 2 lemons , juiced

Method

STEP 1

Put two saucers in the freezer for testing the jam later on. Tip the cherries, sugar and lemon juice into a large, heavy-based saucepan and simmer uncovered over a medium-high heat for 35-50 mins, stirring frequently until thick and glossy.

STEP 2

After 35 mins, spoon a little of the jam onto one of the chilled saucers. Leave for 1 min, press a fingertip into the jam. If it starts the wrinkle, it's ready. If it slides away, continue to boil the jam for 10 mins, then test again on the other saucer.

STEP 3

Spoon the jam into sterilised jars and seal. *Will keep for six months unopened (when stored in a dark, cool place), or opened in the fridge for three months.*

Easy lemon muffins

Prep: 15 mins **Cook:** 30 mins

plus cooling

Easy

Makes 6-8

Ingredients

- 100g unsalted butter , softened
- 100g caster sugar
- 2 eggs , beaten
- 115g self-raising flour

- ¼ tsp baking powder
- 2 lemons , zested and juiced
- 100g yogurt

For the icing

- 150g icing sugar
- 1 lemon , juiced

Method

STEP 1

Line a muffin tin with large muffin cases. Heat the oven to 180C/160C fan/gas 4. Tip all the ingredients in a large bowl and mix until smooth using a wooden spoon or an electric whisk. Spoon tablespoons of the batter into the muffin cases until they're three-quarters full (you can make up to 8, depending on the case size). Bake for 30 mins or until a skewer comes out clean. Leave on a cooling rack to cool completely.

STEP 2

Meanwhile, make the icing. Sieve the icing sugar into a bowl and gradually add lemon juice until you have a thick but pourable icing – you may not need all of the juice. Drizzle over the cooled muffins and serve.

Easy paella

Prep: 10 mins **Cook:** 30 mins

Easy

Serves 4

Ingredients

- 1 tbsp olive oil
- 1 onion, chopped
- 1 tsp each hot smoked paprika and dried thyme
- 300g paella or risotto rice
- 3 tbsp dry sherry or white wine (optional)
- 400g can chopped tomatoes with garlic
- 900ml chicken stock
- 400g frozen seafood mix
- 1 lemon, ½ juiced, ½ cut into wedges
- handful of flat-leaf parsley, roughly chopped

Method

STEP 1

Heat the olive oil in a large frying pan or wok. Add the onion and soften for 5 mins.

STEP 2

Add the smoked paprika, thyme and paella rice, stir for 1 min, then splash in the sherry, if using. Once evaporated, stir in the chopped tomatoes and chicken stock.

STEP 3

Season and cook, uncovered, for about 15 mins, stirring now and again until the rice is almost tender and still surrounded with some liquid.

STEP 4

Stir in the seafood mix and cover with a lid. Simmer for 5 mins, or until the seafood is cooked through and the rice is tender. Squeeze over the lemon juice, scatter over the parsley and serve with the lemon wedges.

Super-easy fruit ice cream

Prep: 20 mins

plus freezing

Easy

Serves 6

Ingredients

- 200g strawberries (as red as you can get), hulled
- 1 large mango, deseeded and peeled
- ¼ lemon, juiced
- 3 very ripe bananas, peeled
- 200g condensed milk
- 600ml double cream
- 4 kiwi fruit, peeled
- sprinkles or finely chopped strawberries and mango, to serve

Method

STEP 1

Mash or purée the strawberries and mango in two separate bowls. In another bowl, add the lemon juice and the banana and mash.

STEP 2

Beat the condensed milk and cream in a large bowl with an electric whisk until thick and quite stiff, a bit like clotted cream. Divide the mixture between the three bowls. Fold a fruit purée into each. Transfer each one into a freezer container and freeze until solid.

STEP 3

Purée the kiwi and sieve out any seeds if you like. Serve a scoop of each ice cream in bowls or sundae dishes and top with the kiwi sauce, sprinkles, or the chopped fruit.

Easy ratatouille

Prep: 25 mins **Cook:** 40 mins

Easy

Serves 4

Ingredients

- 2 aubergines
- 3 medium courgettes
- 2 red peppers
- 2 tbsp olive oil
- 1 large onion , finely diced
- 3 garlic cloves , crushed
- 2 x 400g cans chopped tomatoes
- 1 tsp dried oregano , basil or Italian mixed herbs
- small bunch basil , chopped, plus a few leaves to serve
- 1 tbsp red wine vinegar
- 1-2 tbsp sugar

Method

STEP 1

Dice the aubergine, courgette and pepper into 3cm chunks. Heat the olive oil in a large casserole or deep frying pan over a medium heat. Fry the onion for 10 mins until soft and translucent. Add the chopped veg, turn the heat to high and fry for another 10 mins until softened.

STEP 2

Stir the garlic into the pan, and toss everything together, frying for 1 min more. Tip in the chopped tomatoes, plus half a can of water (200ml), the dried herbs and the chopped basil. Simmer for 20 minutes on a medium heat, stirring occasionally, until the veg is tender and the tomatoes are thick and coating the veg. Season and add the vinegar and sugar to balance the sweet and acidity of the tomatoes. Scatter with the basil leaves, and serve with rustic bread, or pasta.

Easy Christmas turkey

Prep: 20 mins **Cook:** 2 hrs

Easy

Serves 6

Ingredients

- 100g butter, softened
- 3 rosemary sprigs, leaves picked and finely chopped
- 1 turkey (around 4kg, but not more), giblets removed
- 1 garlic bulb
- 1 lemon, halved
- 2 bay leaves
- 2 large banana shallots, unpeeled, cut in half lengthways
- 250ml white wine
- 1 red cabbage (about 900g), cut into 6 wedges
- 500ml good-quality chicken stock
- 1 tsp cornflour (optional)

Method

STEP 1

Take your turkey out of the fridge at least 1 hr before you cook it. Heat oven to 200C/180C fan/gas 6 and beat the butter with the rosemary. Starting from the neck of the turkey, carefully push your fingers underneath the skin until you can get your whole hand between the skin and the breast meat. Trying not to tear the skin as you go, spread the butter inside the pocket, squishing some into the crevice between the thigh and breast meat.

STEP 2

Put the garlic, lemon and bay leaves inside the turkey, then season liberally all over. Put the shallots in your largest flameproof roasting tin and put the turkey on top, breast-side up. Roast for 1 hr, then give it a good baste, pour in the wine and nestle the cabbage wedges in the tin (or underneath the turkey if they won't fit). Return to the oven for another 30 mins – covered with foil if the turkey is looking too brown. The juices should run clear when you pierce the thickest part of the thigh, or a thermometer should read 75C. If not done, carry on cooking for a further 5-10 mins.

STEP 3

Set aside the turkey on a board to rest for 1 hr, transferring the garlic and bay to the roasting tin for the gravy. If you want crispy skin, don't cover the turkey. Wrap the cabbage wedges in two parcels of foil, with a spoonful of the turkey juices, season liberally and return to the bottom of the oven to carry on cooking while the turkey rests.

STEP 4

Spoon away most of the turkey fat, then put the tin on the hob over a medium heat. Mash the veg with the back of a wooden spoon to extract as much flavour as possible, then pour in the stock and reduce the gravy by half. If you want to thicken it, stir in the cornflour mixed with 1 tbsp water. Once happy with the consistency, strain and keep warm until ready to eat.

Easy one-pot chicken casserole

Prep: 5 mins **Cook:** 50 mins

Easy

Serves 4

Ingredients

- 8 bone-in chicken thighs, skin pulled off and discarded
- 1 tbsp oil
- 5 spring onions, sliced
- 2 tbsp plain flour
- 2 chicken stock cubes
- 2 large carrots, cut into batons (no need to peel)
- 400g new potato, halved if large
- 200g frozen peas
- 1 tbsp grainy mustard
- small handful fresh soft herbs, like parsley, chives, dill or tarragon, chopped

Method

STEP 1

Put the kettle on. Fry 8 bone-in chicken thighs in 1 tbsp oil in a casserole dish or wide pan with a lid to quickly brown.

STEP 2

Stir in the whites of 5 spring onions with 2 tbsp plain flour and 2 chicken stock cubes until the flour disappears, then gradually stir in 750ml hot water from the kettle.

STEP 3

Throw in 2 large carrots, in batons and 400g new potatoes, bring to a simmer. Cover and cook for 20 mins.

STEP 4

Take off the lid and simmer for 15 mins more, then throw in 200g peas for another 5 mins.

STEP 5

Season, stir in 1 tbsp grainy mustard, the green spring onion bits, a small handful of fresh soft herbs and some seasoning.

Easy Thai prawn curry

Prep: 5 mins

Cook: 15 mins

Easy

Serves 4

Ingredients

- 1 tbsp vegetable oil
- 1 onion, chopped
- 1 tsp fresh root ginger
- 1-2 tsp Thai red curry paste (we used Sharwood's)
- 400g can chopped tomatoes
- 50g sachet coconut cream
- 400g raw frozen prawns
- coriander, chopped, to serve (optional)

Method

STEP 1

Heat the oil in a medium saucepan. Tip in the onion and ginger, then cook for a few mins until softened. Stir in the curry paste, then cook for 1 min more. Pour over the chopped tomatoes and coconut cream. Bring to the boil, then leave to simmer for 5 mins, adding a little boiling water if the mixture gets too thick.

STEP 2

Tip in the prawns, then cook for 5-10 mins more, depending on how large they are. Serve alongside some plain rice and sprinkle with a little chopped coriander, if you like.

Easy chilli con carne

Prep: 20 mins

Cook: 1 hr

Easy

Serves 4

Ingredients

- 2 tbsp olive oil
- 2 large onions, halved and sliced

- 3 large garlic cloves, chopped
- 2 tbsp mild chilli powder
- 2 tsp ground cumin
- 2 tsp dried oregano
- 1kg pack lean minced beef
- 400g can chopped tomato
- 2 beef stock cubes (we like Just Bouillon)
- 2 large red peppers, deseeded and cut into chunks
- 10 sundried tomatoes
- 3 x 400g cans red kidney beans, drained

Method

STEP 1

Heat oven to 150C/fan 130C/gas 3. Heat the oil, preferably in a large flameproof casserole, and fry the onions for 8 mins. Add the garlic, spices and oregano and cook for 1 min, then gradually add the mince, stirring well until browned. Stir in the tomatoes, add half a can of water, then crumble in the stock and season.

STEP 2

Cover and cook in the oven for 30 mins. Stir in the peppers and sundried tomatoes, then cook for 30 mins more until the peppers are tender. Stir in the beans.

STEP 3

To serve, reheat on the hob until bubbling. Serve with avocado or a big salad with avocado in it, some basmati rice or tortilla chips and a bowl of soured cream.

STEP 4

If you want to use a slow cooker, fry your onions in a pan for 8 mins, then add your garlic, spices and oregano and cook for a minute. Gradually add the mince until it's brown. Tip into your slow cooker with the tomatoes, peppers, sundried tomatoes and beans, crumble in the stock cubes and season to taste. Cook on Low for 8-10 hours, then serve as above.

Pizza Margherita in 4 easy steps

Prep: 25 mins **Cook:** 10 mins

Easy

Makes 2 pizzas, serves 4

Ingredients

For the base

- 300g strong bread flour
- 1 tsp instant yeast (from a sachet or a tub)
- 1 tsp salt
- 1 tbsp olive oil, plus extra for drizzling

For the tomato sauce

- 100ml passata
- handful fresh basil or 1 tsp dried
- 1 garlic clove, crushed

For the topping

- 125g ball mozzarella, sliced
- handful grated or shaved parmesan (or vegetarian alternative)
- handful of cherry tomatoes, halved

To finish

- handful of basil leaves (optional)

Method

STEP 1

Make the base: Put the flour into a large bowl, then stir in the yeast and salt. Make a well, pour in 200ml warm water and the olive oil and bring together with a wooden spoon until you have a soft, fairly wet dough. Turn onto a lightly floured surface and knead for 5 mins until smooth. Cover with a tea towel and set aside. You can leave the dough to rise if you like, but it's not essential for a thin crust.

STEP 2

Make the sauce: Mix the passata, basil and crushed garlic together, then season to taste. Leave to stand at room temperature while you get on with shaping the base.

STEP 3

Roll out the dough: if you've let the dough rise, give it a quick knead, then split into two balls. On a floured surface, roll out the dough into large rounds, about 25cm across, using a rolling pin. The dough needs to be very thin as it will rise in the oven. Lift the rounds onto two floured baking sheets.

STEP 4

Top and bake: heat the oven to 240C/220C fan/gas 8. Put another baking sheet or an upturned baking tray in the oven on the top shelf. Smooth sauce over bases with the back of a spoon. Scatter with cheese and tomatoes, drizzle with olive oil and season. Put one pizza, still on its baking sheet, on top of the preheated sheet or tray. Bake for 8-10 mins until crisp. Serve with a little more olive oil, and basil leaves if using. Repeat step for remaining pizza.

Easy fluffy scones

Prep: 10 mins **Cook:** 12 mins

Easy

Makes 9

Ingredients

- 350g self-raising flour, plus more for dusting
- ¼ tsp salt
- 1 tsp baking powder
- 85g cold butter, cut into cubes
- 4 tbsp golden caster sugar
- 150g pot natural full-fat yogurt
- 4 tbsp full-fat milk
- 1 tsp vanilla extract
- 1 egg beaten with 1 tbsp milk, to glaze

Method

STEP 1

Put a baking sheet in the oven at 220C/200C fan/gas 7. Put the flour, salt and baking powder into a food processor, then whizz in the butter until it disappears. Pulse in the sugar, tip into a large bowl, then make a well in the middle.

STEP 2

Warm the yogurt, milk and vanilla together in the microwave for 1 min or in a pan; it should be hot and may well go a bit lumpy-looking. Tip into the bowl and quickly work into the flour mix using a cutlery knife. As soon as it's all in, stop.

STEP 3

Tip the dough onto a floured surface, then, with floured hands, fold the dough over a few times – just enough to create a smoothish dough. Press out to about 4cm/1½in thick, dip a 7cm cutter into more flour, then stamp out 4 rounds, flouring the cutter each time. Squash the remainder lightly together, then repeat until the dough is used up. Brush tops with egg wash, scatter flour over the hot sheet, then lift the scones on. Bake for 12 mins until risen and golden. Best eaten just-warm, or on the day.

RECIPE TIPS

VARIATIONS

Add 85g sultanas or chopped glacé cherries in with the sugar if you like.

FREEZING TIP

To freeze for up to a month, seal cold baked scones into freezer bags, squeezing out any air. Defrost at room temperature, then heat in a low oven for a few mins to perk them up.

Easy vanilla cake

Prep: 20 mins **Cook:** 1 hr and 20 mins

Easy

Serves 12

Ingredients

- 250g pack unsalted butter, softened, plus extra for greasing
- 250g golden caster sugar
- seeds scraped from 1 vanilla pod or 1 tsp vanilla paste
- 5 large eggs, cracked into a jug
- 85g plain flour
- 100g full-fat Greek yogurt (I used Total)
- 250g self-raising flour
- 3 tbsp semi-skimmed milk

For the syrup

- 50g golden caster sugar
- seeds ½ vanilla pod or ½ tsp vanilla paste

Method

STEP 1

Heat oven to 160C/140C fan/gas 3. Grease a round, deep 20cm tin, then line the base and sides with non-stick baking paper.

STEP 2

Using electric beaters or a tabletop mixer, beat the butter, sugar, vanilla and ¼ tsp salt together until pale and fluffy, then pour in the eggs, one at a time, giving the mix a really good beating before adding the next.

STEP 3

Add 1 tbsp of the plain flour if the mix starts to look slimy rather than fluffy. Beat in the yogurt. Mix the flours; then, using a large metal spoon, fold them into the batter, followed by the milk.

STEP 4

Spoon the mix into the tin and bake for 1 hr 20 mins or until well risen and golden – a skewer inserted into the middle should come out clean.

STEP 5

Meanwhile, make the syrup by gently heating 50ml water with the sugar and vanilla in a pan until the sugar dissolves. Set aside. Once the cake is out of the oven, leave to cool for 30 mins in the tin, then use a skewer to poke holes all over the cake, going right to the bottom. Pour the syrup over, letting it completely soak in after each addition.

STEP 6

Leave to cool completely, then either wrap the cake well or fill and ice it. If you wrap it with baking parchment and cling film, the unfilled cake will keep well for up to 3 days, or in the freezer for up to a month.

STEP 7

For ideas on how to decorate the cake and to try out some variations on this basic cake mixture, have a look at the 'Goes well with' recipes for Simple elegance wedding cake, Birthday bug cake and Summer celebration cake.

RECIPE TIPS

A GOOD, BASIC VANILLA BUTTERCREAM

Put 175g soft unsalted butter into a large bowl. Beat with electric beaters for a few secs until pale. Gradually add 300g sifted icing sugar, a spoonful at a time. Keep beating until mixture is pale and creamy. Beat in seeds from 1 vanilla pod or 1 tsp vanilla paste. Makes enough to cover a 20cm cake. Will keep in fridge for 1 week. Bring back to room temperature and beat well before using.

Easy treacle sponge

Prep: 10 mins - 15 mins **Cook:** 40 mins

Easy

Serves 8

Ingredients

- 250g golden syrup
- zest 1 lemon, plus juice ½ lemon
- 5 tbsp breadcrumb
- 200g pack butter, softened
- 200g golden caster sugar
- 3 medium eggs

- 200g self-raising flour
- 5 tbsp milk

Method

STEP 1

Heat oven to 180C/160C fan/gas 4. Mix the syrup, lemon zest, juice and breadcrumbs and spread over the base of a 1.5 litre baking dish.

STEP 2

Beat the butter and sugar until pale and fluffy, then beat in the eggs, one by one. Stir in the flour and milk and dollop over the syrup. Bake for 35-40 mins until golden and risen, and a skewer poked into the sponge comes out clean-ish. Eat with lots of custard, cream or ice cream and extra dribbles of syrup.

Easy chicken gumbo

Prep: 15 mins **Cook:** 40 mins

Easy

Serves 4

Ingredients

- 2 tbsp olive oil
- 200g smoked bacon lardons
- 1 onion, sliced
- 130g pack Padrón peppers, stalks removed, sliced (or 1 green chilli and 100g green pepper)
- 4 skinless chicken breasts, cut into bite-sized pieces
- 3 tbsp plain flour
- 1 tbsp Cajun spice mix
- 3 garlic cloves, crushed
- 500ml chicken stock
- 175g pack okra, sliced (or 2 courgettes, sliced)
- 500g carton passata
- 2 spring onions, sliced
- cooked rice and black beans, to serve

Method

STEP 1

Heat the oil in a large pan, add the lardons and onion, and fry for 5 mins until the bacon is starting to crisp and the onion is soft. Add the peppers, chicken and flour, and fry for a further 5 mins or until the chicken is golden brown and the flour is starting to take on a a biscuty colour.

STEP 2

Stir in the Cajun spice mix and garlic, then slowly add the chicken stock, stirring all the time. Add the okra, passata and some seasoning and simmer for 20 mins, uncovered, over a medium heat. Stir frequently during cooking to loosen the flour from the base of the pan.

STEP 3

Sprinkle over the spring onions and serve with rice and black beans.

Easy Eccles cakes

Prep: 45 mins **Cook:** 22 mins - 27 mins

plus overnight freezing

Easy

Makes 6

Ingredients

- 50g butter
- 100g light muscovado sugar
- 175g currant
- 50g mixed peel
- zest 2 lemons

For the pastry

- 175g butter , in one block

- 1 tsp ground cinnamon
- 2 pinches ground cloves
- 1 egg white
- 2 tbsp granulated sugar , for sprinkling

- 225g plain flour

Method

STEP 1

The night before, wrap the butter for the pastry in foil and freeze.

STEP 2

The following day, tip your flour into a big bowl with 2 pinches of salt. Hold the butter block in the foil (peeling back a little at a time as you need), then coarsely grate straight into the bowl of flour, dipping the end of the butter into the flour every so often – this helps to stop all the butter clumping together. Use a round-bladed palette or cutlery knife, and lightly stir together. Stir in about 125ml cold water to bring the dough together. Wrap in cling film and chill for 30 mins.

STEP 3

To make the filling, melt the 50g butter, then mix in the muscovado sugar, currants, mixed peel, zest and spices. Heat oven to 200C/180C fan/gas 6.

STEP 4

Roll out the chilled dough on a lightly floured surface to the thickness of a 20p piece. Use a 15cm cutter to stamp out 6 rounds, re-rolling the trimmings if necessary. Divide the filling equally and place in the middle of each round, then brush the edges with a bit of water. Pull up the edges all around each one and pinch to seal.

STEP 5

Turn over the cakes so the seam is underneath, and lightly roll with a floured rolling pin to a flat-ish round. Re-shape to a neat round. Whisk the egg white with a fork until frothy. Use a pastry brush to brush it over the tops of the Eccles cakes, then sprinkle heavily with sugar. Slash the top of each cake 2-3 times to allow the steam to escape. Put on a baking sheet and bake for 20-25 mins until golden and crisp.

Easy meatballs

Prep: 1 hr **Cook:** 40 mins

Easy

Makes 40 meatballs, which will feed a family of 4 twice

Ingredients

- 300g good-quality pork sausage (about 4 large or 8 chipolatas)
- 1 small onion
- 1 carrot
- 1 tbsp dried oregano
- 500g lean beef mince
- 50g parmesan , finely grated, plus extra to serve
- 75g dried breadcrumb
- 1 medium egg
- 1 tbsp olive oil

For the tomato sauce

- 1 carrot (finely grated)
- 2 sticks of celery (grated)
- 1 courgette (coarsely grated)
- 3 garlic cloves (finely grated)
- 2 red peppers
- 1 tbsp olive oil
- 1 tbsp tomato purée
- pinch golden caster sugar
- splash red wine vinegar
- 3 x 400g tins chopped tomatoes
- cooked spaghetti , to serve
- handful basil leaves , snipped

Method

STEP 1

KIDS the writing in bold is for you. GROWN-UPS the rest is for you. **Squeeze some sausages.** Get your child to squeeze all the sausagemeat out of the skins into a large bowl. They can hold the sausages or do it by squashing them on a board.

STEP 2

Get grating. Get your child to coarsely grate the onion and finely grate the carrot. If the onion starts to hurt their eyes, get them to wear goggles, which is good fun. Grating can take a bit of strength, so you may need to help. Tip these vegetables in with the sausages. While you have the grater out, grate the Parmesan, other vegetables and garlic for the sauce, and set aside.

STEP 3

Make a marvellous mix. Next, get your child to add all the other meatball ingredients one by one, except the olive oil, into the bowl and season with black pepper.

STEP 4

Squish everything together. Get the child to squish everything together through their hands until completely mixed. Keep an eye on younger children to make sure that they don't taste any of the raw mix.

STEP 5

Roll meatballs. Children as young as three can now roll the meatball mix into walnut-sized balls, then place them on a board or tray. This mix should make 40 balls – counting these is great way to help teach older children basic division. Cover the meatballs with cling film and have a little tidy up.

STEP 6

Prepare the red peppers. Firstly, peel the peppers with a vegetable peeler, cut off the tops and bottoms and remove the seeds. Cut the peppers in half and children from the age of four can cut the peppers into strips.

STEP 7

Make the sauce. A grown-up will need to help here. Heat the oil in a large saucepan. Add the vegetables and garlic and cook for 5 mins. Stir in the tomato purée, sugar and vinegar, leave for 1 min then tip in the tomatoes and simmer for 5 mins. Get the child to help blitz the sauce with a hand blender. Gently simmer the sauce while you cook the meatballs.

STEP 8

Cook the meatballs. Brown the meatballs in the olive oil on all sides then pop them into the sauce, working in batches if necessary. Simmer the meatballs in the sauce for 15 mins, gently stirring until they are cooked through. It's ready to eat now or cool and freeze in suitable batches for up to 6 months. Serve with spaghetti, some basil and extra Parmesan, if you like.

RECIPE TIPS

ADAPTING FLAVOURS

This is a 'blueprint' recipe that can be adapted to suit your child's taste or introduce new flavours. Ground cumin, paprika or a small pinch of cayenne pepper could be added to the meatballs or you can add different chopped fresh herbs like coriander, parsley, basil or thyme.

HOW TO FREEZE MEATBALLS

Freeze the cooked meatballs into portions that suit your family and clearly label how many portions are in each package. Defrost completely before reheating until very hot, you may need to add a small splash of water if the sauce becomes too thick.

Quiche Lorraine in 4 easy steps

Prep: 20 mins **Cook:** 50 mins

Plus chilling

Easy

Cuts into 8 slices

Ingredients

- flour, for dusting
- 500g block ready-to-roll shortcrust pastry
- 200g smoked streaky bacon, chopped
- 85g medium cheddar, cut into small cubes
- 3 eggs, lightly beaten
- 284ml tub double cream
- pinch grated nutmeg

Method

STEP 1

Roll out pastry and lift into tin: Leave pastry to soften at room temperature so it doesn't crack when rolling. Lightly flour rolling pin and work surface. Gently press top of pastry, from the end closest to you outwards, a few times, turn 90°, then repeat until 1cm thick. Now roll out pastry in one direction only, turning every couple of rolls, to a circle the thickness of a £1 coin. Use the rolling pin to lift pastry up and over tin, floured side facing up.

STEP 2

Line the tin and trim the pastry: Smooth pastry over the base of the tin to remove any pockets of air. Gently ease pastry into the inside edge of tin and against the sides. Trim overhanging pastry with kitchen scissors so pastry rises 1cm above the rim. Roll excess pastry into a small ball and use to press pastry into the fluted edges. Chill for 30 mins, covered with cling film. Any left over can be chilled and reused, or frozen for up to a month.

STEP 3

Bake the pastry case blind: Heat oven to 200C/fan 180C/gas 6. Cut a large piece of baking parchment, then scrunch into a ball. Open it out and use to line chilled pastry case, then tip in baking beans with more against the sides, to support pastry wall when baking. Bake on a baking sheet for 15-20 mins until the sides are crisp and set. Remove from oven and carefully lift paper and beans out. Return pastry to oven and cook for another 5 mins or until the base and sides are golden and crisp.

STEP 4

Fill pastry case and bake Lower oven to 150C/fan 130C/gas 2. Heat a pan, then fry the bacon until golden. Scatter over the pastry base, discarding excess fat, followed by the cheese. Mix eggs, cream and nutmeg together, then half-fill the case. Rest baking sheet on an oven shelf, then pour in the rest of the mixture. Bake for 30-35 mins or until just set. Remove and allow to cool for 10 mins.

RECIPE TIPS

PROBLEM SOLVING

The pastry shrank during baking: If you don't chill your pastry for long enough, the butter will start to melt during baking before the pastry has time to set, causing shrinkage. Chill the pastry for at least 30 mins before baking – plus, if you trim the pastry so that it is above the rim, it won't matter if it shrinks slightly.

THE COOKED PASTRY CASE CRACKED

Pastry that is rolled out too much becomes overworked and too elastic. As a result, it can spring back during baking or little cracks form. Get the pastry to a pliable texture before you start rolling, then do lots of gentle rolls and turns as opposed to a few forceful ones. Plug any small cracks with a little leftover pastry before pouring in the custard.

Easy Scotch eggs

Prep: 20 mins **Cook:** 20 mins

Easy

Makes 4

Ingredients

- 5 large eggs
- 300g good-quality pork sausage, skinned
- 1 tsp black peppercorns, crushed
- 140g cooked ham, shredded
- 25g sage, apple & onion stuffing mix
- 1 tsp chopped sage
- 1 tsp chopped thyme
- 1 tsp chopped parsley
- 100g plain flour, seasoned, plus extra for dusting
- 100g dried breadcrumbs
- sunflower oil, for frying
- piccalilli, to serve

Method

STEP 1

Bring a pan of salted water to a rapid boil, then lower four of the eggs into the pan and simmer for 7 mins 30 secs exactly. Scoop out and place in a bowl of iced water, cracking the shells a little (this makes them easier to peel later). Leave them to cool completely, then peel and set aside. *Can be boiled the day before.*

STEP 2

Put the sausagemeat, pepper, ham, stuffing and herbs in a small bowl, mix to combine, then divide into four equal balls. Squash one of the balls between a piece of cling film until it's as flat as possible. One at a time, lightly flour each cooked egg, then use the cling film to help roll the sausagemeat around the egg to completely encase. Repeat with the remaining sausageballs and eggs.

STEP 3

Beat the remaining egg and put on a plate. Put the flour and breadcrumbs on two separate plates. Roll the encased eggs in the flour, then the beaten egg and finally the breadcrumbs. *Can be prepared up to a day in advance.*

STEP 4

To cook the eggs, heat 5cm of the oil in a wide saucepan or wok until it reaches 160C on a cooking thermometer or until a few breadcrumbs turn golden after 10 secs in the oil. Depending on the size of your pan, lower as many eggs as you can into the oil, and cook for 8-10 mins until golden and crispy. Drain on kitchen paper, leave to cool a little, then serve halved with some piccalilli.

Easy roast beef

Prep: 15 mins **Cook:** 1 hr

Plus resting

Easy

Serves 4

Ingredients

- 1 tsp plain flour
- 1 tsp mustard powder
- 950g beef top rump joint (see tip below)
- 1 onion, cut into 8 wedges
- 500g carrots, halved lengthways

For the gravy

- 1 tbsp plain flour
- 250ml beef stock

Method

STEP 1

Heat oven to 240C/220C fan/gas 9.

STEP 2

Mix 1 tsp plain flour and 1 tsp mustard powder with some seasoning, then rub all over the 950g beef top rump joint.

STEP 3

Put 1 onion, cut into 8 wedges, and 500g carrots, halved lengthways, into a roasting tin and sit the beef on top, then cook for 20 mins.

STEP 4

Reduce oven to 190C/170C fan/gas 5 and continue to cook the beef for 30 mins if you like it rare, 40 mins for medium and 1 hr for well done.

STEP 5

Remove the beef and carrots from the oven, place onto warm plates or platters and cover with foil to keep warm.

STEP 6

Let the beef rest for 30 mins while you turn up the oven to cook your Yorkshire puds and finish the potatoes.

STEP 7

For the gravy, put the tin with all the meat juices and onions back onto the hob.

STEP 8

Stir in 1 tbsp plain flour, scraping all the stuck bits off the bottom of the tin. Cook for 30 seconds, then slowly stir in 250ml beef stock, little by little.

STEP 9

Bubble to a nice gravy, season, then serve with the beef, carved into slices, carrots and all the other trimmings.

RECIPE TIPS

A NEW CUT OF BEEF

You might not have tried top rump before, but it's a very economical joint of beef, so makes a good-value Sunday lunch. Look for British meat, well aged. It's best eaten pink as this will keep it tender.

Easy-bake bread

Prep: 30 mins **Cook:** 35 mins

Plus 1-2 hrs proving

Easy

Makes 1 large loaf

Ingredients

- 500g strong bread flour
- 7g sachet fast-action dried yeast
- 1 tsp salt
- 300ml hand-hot water
- 2 tbsp sunflower oil
- 1 tbsp honey

Method

STEP 1

Tip the flour into a bowl and mix in the yeast with the salt. Stir in the water, oil and honey. Now bring together to make a soft dough – I use my hands, but a wooden spoon or knife from the cutlery drawer is fine. Tip onto a lightly floured surface and knead for 10 mins. It is worth putting in the time to do this as it will pay off later with lovely airy bread.

STEP 2

Don't keep adding flour, a wet dough is better than a dry one, which will bake to a tough texture, so if you don't like the dough sticking to your hands, lightly oil them. If you are adding flavourings, knead them in gently now.

STEP 3

Turn the dough into an oiled 1kg bread tin and cover with oiled cling film (or better still, a free unused shower cap from your last hotel stay!). Put in a warm place until the bread fills the tin, it should take between 1-2 hrs.

STEP 4

Uncover and bake your bread at 200C/180C fan/gas 6 for 30-35 mins until golden. Tip out of the tin and tap the base of the loaf. It should sound hollow when fully cooked. If not cooked, put loaf back in the oven out of the tin and test again after 10 mins. Cool.

Family meals: Easy lamb tagine

Prep: 10 mins **Cook:** 2 hrs and 10 mins

Easy

Serves a family of 4-6 or makes 6-8 toddler meals

Ingredients

- 2 tbsp olive oil
- 1 onion, finely diced
- 2 carrots, finely diced (about 150g)
- 500g diced leg of lamb
- 2 fat cloves garlic, crushed
- ½ tsp cumin
- ½ tsp ground ginger
- ¼ tsp saffron strands
- 1 tsp ground cinnamon
- 1 tbsp clear honey
- 100g soft dried apricot, quartered
- 1 low-salt vegetable stock cube
- 1 small butternut squash, peeled, seeds removed and cut into 1cm dice

- steamed couscous or rice, to serve
- chopped parsley and toasted pine nuts, to serve (optional)

Method

STEP 1

Heat the olive oil in a heavy-based pan and add the onion and carrot. Cook for 3- 4 mins until softened.

STEP 2

Add the diced lamb and brown all over. Stir in the garlic and all the spices and cook for a few mins more or until the aromas are released.

STEP 3

Add the honey and apricots, crumble in the stock cube and pour over roughly 500ml boiling water or enough to cover the meat. Give it a good stir and bring to the boil. Turn down to a simmer, put the lid on and cook for 1 hour.

STEP 4

Remove the lid and cook for a further 30 mins, then stir in the squash. Cook for 20 – 30 mins more until the squash is soft and the lamb is tender. Serve alongside rice or couscous and sprinkle with parsley and pine nuts, if using.

Really easy roast chicken

Prep: 25 mins **Cook:** 1 hr and 20 mins

Easy

Serves 4 with leftover chicken

Ingredients

- 1 whole chicken , about 1.5kg
- 1 lemon , halved
- 2 garlic cloves
- thyme or rosemary sprig, if you have it
- 50g soft butter
- 800g very small salad potato , such as Charlotte, halved if you can only find large ones
- 350g small Chantenay carrot , or 3-4 regular carrots. cut into chunks
- 1 tbsp olive oil
- 300ml chicken stock

- 1 tbsp low-salt soy sauce

Method

STEP 1

KIDS: The writing in bold is for you. ADULTS: The rest is for you. **Cut the string off the chicken.** Heat oven to 220C/200C fan/gas 7. Get your child to use a pair of scissors to cut the elastic or string holding the chicken together.

STEP 2

Stuff the chicken. Stuff the lemon halves in the cavity of the chicken with the garlic and herb sprig (if using).

STEP 3

Time to get your hands mucky. Sit the chicken in a large roasting tin and use your hands to smear the butter all over it.

STEP 4

Easy-peasy vegetables. Tip the carrots and potatoes into a large bowl, drizzle over the oil and toss everything together with your hands.

STEP 5

Scatter the vegetables around the chicken. Scatter the vegetables in an even layer around the chicken, then season everything. Put the chicken in the oven and roast for 30 mins. Remove from the oven and give the vegetables a stir, reduce the heat to 200C/180C fan/gas 6, then return to the oven for 50 mins more.

STEP 6

Test if the chicken is cooked. Remove the chicken from the oven. Using a cloth, pull the leg – if it easily comes away from the body, there is no sign of pink and the juices run clear, the chicken is cooked. If you have a digital cooking thermometer, it should read above 70C. Take the chicken out of the tin.

STEP 7

Make a lemony sauce. Scoop the vegetables into a serving dish. Using a spoon or a pair of tongs, remove the garlic, lemon and herbs from the chicken and put them in the roasting tin. Squash them down well with a potato masher to release all the juice from the lemons.

STEP 8

Strain the sauce. Pour in the chicken stock and soy sauce and give it all a good stir. Get the child to hold a sieve over a jug while you lift up the pan and strain the juices into the jug. If you want it piping hot, reheat in a pan or in the microwave.

RECIPE TIPS

WHAT KIDS LEARN FROM MAKING REALLY EASY ROAST CHICKEN

Roasting: At its most basic, roasting is nothing more than putting something in the oven to cook. Seeing the process happen from start to finish gives a child a greater understanding of how so many family meals end up cooked and on the table. **Using the oven:** As there is no direct flame, using the oven is the first way kids will progress to cook alone. It's good for them to know how it works and how hot it can get – if your oven has a clear glass door, then they can even watch things as they cook.

Bread in four easy steps

Prep: 15 mins **Cook:** 35 mins

Plus rising

Easy

Cuts into 8 thick slices

Ingredients

- 500g granary, strong wholewheat or white bread flour (I used granary)
- 7g sachet fast-action dried yeast
- 1 tsp salt
- 2 tbsp olive oil
- 1 tbsp clear honey

Method

STEP 1

Tip the flour, yeast and salt into a large bowl and mix together with your hands. Stir 300ml hand-hot water with the oil and honey, then stir into the dry ingredients to make a soft dough.

STEP 2

Turn the dough out onto a lightly floured surface and knead for 5 mins, until the dough no longer feels sticky, sprinkling with a little more flour if you need it.

STEP 3

Oil a 900g loaf tin and put the dough in the tin, pressing it in evenly. Put in a large plastic food bag and leave to rise for 1 hr, until the dough has risen to fill the tin and it no longer springs back when you press it with your finger.

STEP 4

Heat oven to 200C/fan 180C/gas 6. Make several slashes across the top of the loaf with a sharp knife, then bake for 30-35 mins until the loaf is risen and golden. Tip it out onto a cooling rack and tap the base of the bread to check it is cooked. It should sound hollow. Leave to cool.

Cheese soufflé in 4 easy steps

Prep: 15 mins **Cook:** 30 mins

Plus cooling time

Easy

Serves 4

Ingredients

- 50g butter, plus extra for greasing
- 25g breadcrumbs
- 50g plain flour
- 1 tsp mustard powder
- 300ml milk
- 4 eggs
- 100g grated extra-strong cheddar (blue cheese, goat's cheese and smoked cheeses also work well)

Method

STEP 1

Preparing the soufflé dish: Heat oven to 200C/fan 180C/gas 6 and place a baking sheet on the middle shelf. Butter a 15cm soufflé dish generously, then sprinkle in the breadcrumbs and rotate the dish to ensure the butter is evenly coated. Tip out any excess breadcrumbs.

STEP 2

Making a thick white sauce: In a pan, melt the butter over a medium heat; stir in the flour and mustard. Cook, stirring, for 1 min. Take off the heat and gradually stir in the milk, mixing it in thoroughly before adding more. Return to the heat and stir continuously until very thick (around 10 mins). Transfer to a bowl and allow to cool. Crack the eggs, placing the whites into a clean bowl and stirring the yolks into the sauce. Stir in cheddar and season well.

STEP 3

Adding the egg whites: Use a clean whisk to beat the egg whites until peaks form that just hold their shape (electric is best as it will make the job much quicker). Then take a metal spoon and gently stir the whipped whites into the white sauce in a figure of eight.

STEP 4

Top-hatting: Spoon the mixture into the dish. Run a cutlery knife around the edge to create a 'top hat' effect; this ensures the soufflé rises above the rim and doesn't stick. Place on the baking sheet and bake for 25-30 mins until the top is golden and risen and has a slight wobble. Serve immediately.

STEP 5

EQUIPMENT: 15cm soufflé dish, saucepan, 2 large mixing bowls, wooden spoon, spatula, baking sheet, large metal spoon, measuring jug, grater, electric whisk, cutlery knife.

RECIPE TIPS

VANILLA

Line dish with butter and caster sugar, then make the soufflé as above, adding the seeds from 1 vanilla pod and 100g caster sugar and omitting the cheese and mustard.

HASN'T RISEN?

Why? The egg whites may have been overwhisked (see below) or folded in too vigorously, causing the air to be knocked out of them. And if the oven door is opened before the 25 minutes is up, this would also cause the soufflé to collapse.

MAKE INDIVIDUAL ONES

Fill six small ramekins up to three-quarters full, top-hat and then bake as before for 10-15 mins.

MOLTEN CHOCOLATE

Line dish with ground almonds. Replace 2 tbsp of the flour with cocoa powder; omit mustard and cheese. Bake. Meanwhile, make a sauce by heating 142ml carton cream, pouring over 100g chopped dark chocolate and stirring until smooth. Drizzle onto the soufflé to serve.

RUNNY INSIDE?

There should be a little runny mixture in the very centre of the soufflé, but if it is completely runny inside it will need to cook for longer.

Easy chocolate brownie cake

Prep: 15 mins - 20 mins **Cook:** 45 mins

Easy

Serves 10

Ingredients

- 175g unsalted butter, plus extra for greasing
- 225g dark chocolate, broken into pieces
- 200g caster sugar
- 3 medium eggs, separated
- 65g plain flour
- 50g chopped pecan nuts

Method

STEP 1

Heat oven to 180C/fan 160C/gas 4. Butter a 20-25cm cake tin and line with greaseproof paper.

STEP 2

Place 175g/6oz of the chocolate, plus the butter and sugar in a heavy-based pan and heat gently until melted, stirring occasionally. Leave to cool.

STEP 3

Whisk the egg yolks into the chocolate mixture, then add the flour, nuts and the remaining chocolate.

STEP 4

Whisk the egg whites until they form soft peaks, then gently, but thoroughly, fold into the chocolate mixture.

STEP 5

Pour into the prepared tin and bake in the centre of the oven for about 35-40 mins until crusty on top. Leave to cool, then run a knife around the sides and remove from the tin. Dust with icing sugar and serve warm with custard or ice cream or cold with cream.

Easy chicken casserole

Prep: 20 mins **Cook:** 1 hr

Easy

Serves 4

Ingredients

- 2 tbsp sunflower oil
- 400g boneless, skinless chicken thigh , trimmed and cut into chunks
- 1 onion , finely chopped
- 3 carrots , finely chopped
- 3 celery sticks, finely chopped
- 2 thyme sprigs or ½ tsp dried
- 1 bay leaf , fresh or dried
- 600ml vegetable or chicken stock
- 2 x 400g / 14oz cans haricot beans , drained
- chopped parsley , to serve

Method

STEP 1

Heat the oil in a large pan, add the chicken, then fry until lightly browned. Add the veg, then fry for a few mins more. Stir in the herbs and stock. Bring to the boil. Stir well, reduce the heat, then cover and cook for 40 mins, until the chicken is tender.

STEP 2

Stir the beans into the pan, then simmer for 5 mins. Stir in the parsley and serve with crusty bread.

Easy raspberry & ginger trifle cheesecake

Prep: 25 mins

plus chilling, no cook

Easy

Serves 8 - 10

Ingredients

- 150ml Marsala, madeira or medium-sweet Sherry
- 2 x 300g packs cream cheese
- 600ml double cream
- 50g icing sugar , sifted
- 2 x 250g packs gingernut biscuits

- 2 x 200g punnets of raspberries

Method

STEP 1

Put 50ml of the alcohol in a bowl with the cream cheese and beat with an electric whisk until smooth. Add the cream and sugar and beat again until well mixed and softly whipped.

STEP 2

Using a pastry brush, quickly brush a gingernut biscuit with a little of the remaining alcohol. Stack, brushed-side down, on a cake plate or stand, then repeat to make a large round base of biscuits. Spread over a layer of cream, squish in some raspberries, then repeat with another layer of biscuits, pressing down slightly to stick. Repeat layers, finishing with a fourth layer of cream and raspberries. Cover with an upturned mixing bowl, or very loosely with cling film, then chill until ready to serve. It's good after 2 hrs, but could be made the day before, too. Serve with a sprinkling of crushed gingernut biscuit.

Easy biscotti

Prep: 20 mins **Cook:** 50 mins

plus cooling

Easy

Serves 20

Ingredients

- 300g plain flour
- 100g caster sugar
- 50g light brown soft sugar
- 1½ tsp baking powder
- 80g vegetable oil
- 1 large egg
- 2 tsp vanilla extract
- milk or dark chocolate , melted, to decorate (optional)

Method

STEP 1

Heat the oven to 180C/160C fan/gas 4, and line a baking tray with baking parchment. Put the flour, sugars, baking powder and a large pinch of salt in a large bowl and stir together.

STEP 2

In a separate bowl, whisk together the oil, egg, vanilla and 3 tbsp hot water. Gradually mix the wet ingredients into the dry until the mixture comes together into a dough. Gently knead the dough until smooth – it will be quite dry, so add another 1 tbsp water if it's too difficult to knead after a few minutes. Divide the dough into two equal pieces, shaping each into a 25 x 8cm log. Put the logs on the prepared baking tray and bake for 25-30 mins. Remove from the oven and leave to cool on the tray for around 15 mins.

STEP 3

Using a sharp knife, cut the slightly cooled logs into 1-2cm-thick slices crosswise. Return the biscotti to the lined baking tray and bake for 15-20 mins more (the oven should still be at 180C/160C fan/gas 4), turning the tray around halfway through. Leave to cool slightly on the tray, then transfer the biscotti to a wire rack and leave to cool completely. If you like, dip one end of each biscotti into some melted chocolate, then leave to set on a baking tray lined with baking parchment. *Will keep in an airtight container for up to five days.*

Recipe tip

You can use the biscotti in a tiramisu in place of sponge fingers. Simply soften the biscotti in some hot coffee – they'll retain their texture and add delicious flavour.

Really easy lemonade

Prep: 10 mins

No cook

Easy

Ingredients

3 unwaxed lemons, roughly chopped

140g caster sugar

1l cold water

Method

STEP 1

Tip the lemons, sugar and half the water into a food processor and blend until the lemon is finely chopped.

STEP 2

Pour the mixture into a sieve over a bowl, then press through as much juice as you can. Top up with the remaining water and serve with plain ice or frozen with slices of lemon and lime.

Easy meatloaf recipe

Prep: 20 mins **Cook:** 1 hr

Easy

Cuts into 8-10 slices

Ingredients

- 2 slices fresh white bread, crusts removed
- 500g pack minced pork
- 1 onion, roughly chopped
- 1 garlic clove, roughly chopped
- big handful of parsley
- 1 tbsp fresh chopped oregano or 1 tsp dried
- 4 tbsp freshly grated parmesan
- 1 egg, beaten
- 8 slices prosciutto

Method

STEP 1

Heat the oven to 190C/fan 170C/gas 5. Put bread in processor and blitz to make crumbs, then tip into a bowl with the pork.

STEP 2

Tip the onion, garlic and herbs into the food processor and process until finely chopped. Add to the bowl with the parmesan and egg. Finely chop 2 slices of the prosciutto and add to the mix with some salt and pepper. Mix well with a fork or your hands.

STEP 3

Use the rest of the prosciutto to line a 1.5 litre loaf tin. Spoon in the meatloaf mix and press down well. Flip the overhanging prosciutto over the top, then put the loaf tin into a roasting tray.

STEP 4

Pour hot water from the kettle into the roasting tray to come halfway up the loaf tin and bake for 1 hr until loaf shrinks from the sides of tin.

STEP 5

Cool in the tin for 10 mins, then drain off any excess liquid and turn out onto a board. Cut into thick slices and serve warm or cold with salad.

Easy Christmas pudding ice cream

Prep: 15 mins

plus freezing

Easy

Serves 10

Ingredients

- 4 large egg yolks
- 100g caster sugar
- 175g leftover Christmas pudding
- 2-3 tbsp brandy or orange liquer
- 300ml pot double cream

Method

STEP 1

Whisk the egg yolks and sugar with an electric whisk for 10 mins until pale and thick. Break up the Christmas pudding with a fork and stir it into the egg mixture so it is evenly distributed, then pour in the brandy and mix again.

STEP 2

In a separate bowl, whip the cream until it holds soft peaks, then fold it into the mixture with a large metal spoon. Pour into a freezer-proof container, cover well and freeze for several hours until set.

Easy Easter nests

Prep: 25 mins **Cook:** 8 mins

Plus chilling

Easy

Makes 12

Ingredients

- 200g milk chocolate , broken into pieces
- 85g shredded wheat , crushed

- 2 x 100g bags mini chocolate eggs

You'll also need

- cupcake cases

Method

STEP 1

Melt the chocolate in a small bowl placed over a pan of barely simmering water. Pour the chocolate over the shredded wheat and stir well to combine.

STEP 2

Spoon the chocolate wheat into 12 cupcake cases and press the back of a teaspoon in the centre to create a nest shape. Place 3 mini chocolate eggs on top of each nest. Chill the nests in the fridge for 2 hrs until set.

Easy apple fruit cake

Prep: 15 mins **Cook:** 1 hr

Easy

Cuts into 12 slices

Ingredients

- 200g butter, softened plus extra for greasing
- 200g dark muscovado sugar
- 3 eggs, beaten
- 1 tbsp black treacle
- 200g self-raising flour
- 2 tsp mixed spice
- 1 tsp baking powder
- 2 eating apples, grated (approx 100g each)
- 300g mixed sultanas and raisins

Method

STEP 1

Heat oven to 180C/fan 160C/gas 4. Butter and line the bottom of a deep, round 20cm cake tin with greaseproof paper. Beat the first seven ingredients together in a large bowl (electric hand-beaters are best for this), until pale and thick. Using a large metal spoon, gently fold in the fruit until evenly combined.

STEP 2

Spoon the batter into the tin and bake for 50 mins-1 hr or until the cake is dark golden, springy to the touch and has shrunk away from the tin slightly. A skewer inserted into the centre will come out clean when it's ready. Cool completely before decorating. Will keep, wrapped in an airtight container or iced, for up to a week, or can be frozen un-iced for up to a month – defrost fully before decorating.

Easy baked pears with amaretti

Prep: 5 mins **Cook:** 20 mins

Easy

Serves 4

Ingredients

- 4 ripe pears
- 100g ricotta
- ½ tsp cinnamon
- 4 tbsp clear honey , plus extra to serve
- 8 crisp amaretti biscuits

Method

STEP 1

Cut each pear in half, then place on a large baking tray. Use a teaspoon to scoop out the cores and make a dip in the centre of each pear. If your pears are firm, you may need to use a sharp knife to do this. Dollop about 1 heaped tsp ricotta into each dip, then sprinkle over the cinnamon and drizzle with a little honey.

STEP 2

Heat oven to 190C/fan 170C/gas 5, then roast the pears for 10 mins. Tip the biscuits into a food bag and use a rolling pin to lightly crush them. Remove the pears from the oven, then scatter the crumbs over each pear. Return to the oven for another 10 mins or until the pears are soft and the biscuit golden brown. Serve drizzled with honey.

RECIPE TIPS

MAKE A WINTER TRIFLE

Drain 2 x 400g cans pear halves, reserving a little juice. Mix the pears with the honey and 6 of the amaretti biscuits in a large serving bowl. Splash with a little of the reserved juice. Scatter with the cinnamon, then spoon over a 600ml pot ready-made custard. Beat together the ricotta, a 142ml pot double cream and icing sugar to taste, then spoon over the custard layer. Sprinkle with the remaining crushed biscuits.

Easy white bread

Prep: 20 mins **Cook:** 25 mins - 30 mins

Plus 2 hours proving

Easy

Makes 1 loaf

Ingredients

- 500g strong white flour, plus extra for dusting
- 2 tsp salt
- 7g sachet fast-action yeast
- 3 tbsp olive oil
- 300ml water

Method

STEP 1

Mix 500g strong white flour, 2 tsp salt and a 7g sachet of fast-action yeast in a large bowl.

STEP 2

Make a well in the centre, then add 3 tbsp olive oil and 300ml water, and mix well. If the dough seems a little stiff, add another 1-2 tbsp water and mix well.

STEP 3

Tip onto a lightly floured work surface and knead for around 10 mins.

STEP 4

Once the dough is satin-smooth, place it in a lightly oiled bowl and cover with cling film. Leave to rise for 1 hour until doubled in size or place in the fridge overnight.

STEP 5

Line a baking tray with baking parchment. Knock back the dough (punch the air out and pull the dough in on itself) then gently mould the dough into a ball.

STEP 6

Place it on the baking parchment to prove for a further hour until doubled in size.

STEP 7

Heat oven to 220C/fan 200C/gas 7.

STEP 8

Dust the loaf with some extra flour and cut a cross about 6cm long into the top of the loaf with a sharp knife.

STEP 9

Bake for 25-30 mins until golden brown and the loaf sounds hollow when tapped underneath. Cool on a wire rack.

Easy beef hotpot

Total time : 45 mins **Ready in 40-45 minutes**

Easy

Serves 5 - 6

Ingredients

- 2 onions
- 300g carrots
- 1kg potatoes
- 450g lean minced beef
- 2 beef stock cubes
- 400g can baked beans
- splash of Worcestershire sauce
- handful of roughly chopped parsley (optional)

Method

STEP 1

Cut each onion into eight wedges. Roughly chop the carrots and cut the potatoes into large chunks. Put the kettle on.

STEP 2

Heat a large non-stick pan, add the mince and fry quickly, stirring all the time, until evenly browned. Crumble in the stock cubes and mix well. Add the prepared vegetables, stir them around, then pour in 900ml/1½ pints of hot water from the kettle. Bring to the boil.

STEP 3

Reduce the heat, cover and simmer for 25-30 minutes, until the veg are tender. Stir in the baked beans and a generous splash of Worcestershire sauce and heat through. Taste and add salt and pepper if necessary.

STEP 4

Scatter over the parsley, then ladle the hotpot into bowls. Put the Worcestershire sauce bottle on the table in case anyone fancies a bit more spice.

Easy Thai green chicken curry

Prep: 25 mins **Cook:** 30 mins

More effort

Serves 4

Ingredients

- 2 x 400g cans coconut milk
- 3 tbsp green curry paste (see 'Goes well with' recipe below - you will need more if you buy ready-made paste)
- 800g skinless chicken thigh, each thigh cut into three
- 6 lime leaves, stalks removed, shredded
- 3 lemongrass stalks, outer leaves removed and inner stalk finely chopped
- 25g galangal, sliced
- 1 tbsp palm sugar
- 1 tbsp fish sauce
- handful pea aubergines or ½ aubergine, diced
- small bunch Thai basil

Method

STEP 1

Scrape the thick, fatty part of the coconut milk into a warm wok. Cook it slowly, stirring all the time, until it starts to bubble and sizzle and just begins to split. Add the green curry paste and cook for 3-4 mins until the paste starts to release the true smell of South-east Asia.

STEP 2

Add the chicken and stir well, coating it all in the paste. Add the rest of the coconut milk, lime leaves, lemongrass, galangal, palm sugar and half the fish sauce. Let the sauce bubble for about 10 mins, until the oil in the coconut milk starts to come through to the surface and the chicken is cooked. Add the pea aubergines and the rest of the fish sauce and cook for 5 mins more. Scatter on the Thai basil and serve with some jasmine rice.

Easy turkey paella

Cook: 18 mins - 24 mins

Easy

Serves 4

Ingredients

- 205g jar of paella paste
- 300g paella rice
- 300g pack stir-fry vegetables (without beansprouts)
- 130g pack roast turkey slices

Method

STEP 1

Heat 1 tbsp olive oil in a large sauté pan. Fry the paella paste for 1-2 mins, then tip in the rice and cook for 2 mins more. Add 800ml boiling water, simmer for 12-15 mins or until the liquid has been absorbed, then season to taste.

STEP 2

In another pan, fry the veg in 1 tbsp olive oil on a high heat for 1-2 mins. Add 50ml water, cover and steam for 2-3 mins. Tear the turkey into bite-sized pieces and stir through the rice with the veg.

Easy turkey paella

Cook: 18 mins - 24 mins

Easy

Serves 4

Ingredients

- 205g jar of paella paste
- 300g paella rice
- 300g pack stir-fry vegetables (without beansprouts)
- 130g pack roast turkey slices

Method

STEP 1

Heat 1 tbsp olive oil in a large sauté pan. Fry the paella paste for 1-2 mins, then tip in the rice and cook for 2 mins more. Add 800ml boiling water, simmer for 12-15 mins or until the liquid has been absorbed, then season to taste.

STEP 2

In another pan, fry the veg in 1 tbsp olive oil on a high heat for 1-2 mins. Add 50ml water, cover and steam for 2-3 mins. Tear the turkey into bite-sized pieces and stir through the rice with the veg.

Easy lentil curry

Prep: 5 mins **Cook:** 45 mins

Easy

Serves 4

Ingredients

- 2 tbsp sunflower oil
- 2 medium onions, cut into rough wedges
- 4 tbsp curry paste
- 850ml vegetable stock
- 750g stewpack frozen vegetables
- 100g red lentil
- 200g basmati rice
- turmeric
- handful of raisins and roughly chopped parsley
- poppadums and mango chutney, to serve

Method

STEP 1

Heat the oil in a large pan. Add the onions and cook over a high heat for about 8 minutes or until they are golden brown. Stir in the curry paste and cook for a minute. Slowly pour in a little of the stock so it sizzles, scraping any bits from the bottom of the pan. Gradually pour in the rest of the stock.

STEP 2

Stir the frozen vegetables, cover and simmer for 5 minutes. Add the lentils and simmer for a further 15-20 minutes or until the vegetables and lentils are cooked.

STEP 3

While the curry is simmering, cook the rice according to the packet instructions, adding the turmeric to the cooking water. Drain well.

STEP 4

Season the curry with salt, toss in a handful of raisins and chopped parsley, then serve with the rice, poppadums and chutney.

Easy garlic sauce

Prep: 5 mins

No cook

Easy

Serves 8

Ingredients

- 3 garlic cloves
- 150g Greek yogurt
- 1 lemon , juiced
- 2 tbsp tahini
- handful of chopped mint

Method

STEP 1

Crush the garlic cloves.

STEP 2

Combine the crushed garlic with the Greek yogurt, lemon juice, tahini and chopped mint.

RECIPE TIPS

TZATZIKI WITH TAHINI

Coarsely grate some cucumber and mix with a pinch of salt. Leave to rest for a minute, then squeeze out the liquid and pat dry. Stir this through any leftover garlic sauce with some chopped mint, if you like.

Easy homemade chocolate bark

Prep: 15 mins **Cook:** 10 mins

plus setting

Easy

Makes 1 large slab (will fill 4 medium gift bags)

Ingredients

- 400g milk or dark chocolate, broken into pieces
- 100g white chocolate, broken into pieces
- 75g biscuits, of your choice, broken into pieces
- 2 tbsp sprinkles, chopped nuts or sweets

Method

STEP 1

Melt the milk or dark chocolate in a large heatproof bowl set over a pan of simmering water. Remove from the heat, then melt the white chocolate in the same way. Or, melt the chocolates in the microwave in short bursts.

STEP 2

Line a baking tray or sheet with baking parchment. Use a baking sheet if you want thinner shards of bark, or a smaller tray for fewer, chunkier pieces.

STEP 3

Pour the melted milk or dark chocolate over the prepared sheet or tray, then tip side to side to spread the chocolate out to your desired shape and thickness. Spoon over teaspoonfuls of the white chocolate, reserving a little, then use the tip of a knife or a skewer to swirl the white chocolate through the milk or dark.

STEP 4

Scatter over the biscuit pieces, then drizzle over the remaining white chocolate in a spiral pattern. Scatter over the sprinkles, nuts or sweets, then leave in a cool place to set fully. Cut or break into pieces and wrap.

Easy chicken tagine

Prep: 10 mins **Cook:** 40 mins

Easy

Serves 4

Ingredients

- 2 tbsp olive oil
- 8 skinless boneless chicken thighs, halved if large
- 1 onion, chopped
- 2 tsp grated fresh root ginger
- pinch saffron or tumeric
- 1 tbsp honey
- 400g carrot, cut into sticks
- small bunch parsley, roughly chopped
- lemon wedges, to serve

Method

STEP 1

Heat the oil in a large, wide pan with a lid, add the chicken, then fry quickly until lightly coloured. Add the onion and ginger, then fry for a further 2 mins.

STEP 2

Add 150ml water, the saffron, honey and carrots, season, then stir well. Bring to the boil, cover tightly, then simmer for 30 mins until the chicken is tender. Uncover and increase the heat for about 5 mins to reduce the sauce a little. Sprinkle with parsley and serve with lemon wedges for squeezing over.

RECIPE TIPS

TIP: CHICKEN BREASTS

You can make this dish using 4 boneless, skinless chicken breasts instead of thighs. Simply cut them in half and reduce the simmering time to 15 mins.

Family meals: Easy beef stew with sweet potato topping

Prep: 15 mins **Cook:** 2 hrs and 30 mins

Easy

Serves a family of 4 - 6 or makes 6-8 toddler meals

Ingredients

- 1 tbsp olive oil
- 1 onion, finely chopped
- 2 carrots, finely diced (about 130g)
- 1-2 sticks celery, finely diced (about 130g)
- 2 fat cloves garlic, crushed
- 400-500g braising steak
- 1 tsp ground cinnamon
- 1 low-salt beef stock cube
- 2 tbsp tomato purée
- 1 x 25g pack parsley, stalks and leaves finely chopped separately
- 1kg sweet potatoes, peeled and diced
- knob of butter
- handful grated cheddar

Method

STEP 1

Heat the olive oil in a heavy-based pan. Add the onions and cook for 2 mins, then add the carrot and celery and cook until softened. Add a little water if the mixture sticks.

STEP 2

Add the braising steak and cook until browned, then stir in the garlic and cinnamon and cook for a further 1 – 2 mins until the aromas are released.

STEP 3

Add the stock cube to 500ml boiling water and stir into the meat, along with the tomato purée and parsley stalks. Bring to the boil and simmer covered for 1 hour, then take off the lid and simmer for another hour or until the meat is very tender. Stir in the chopped parsley leaves.

STEP 4

Transfer the stew into a medium-sized ceramic dish (that would be big enough for four adults), or into 6 - 8 large ramekins for make-ahead toddler portions.

STEP 5

Meanwhile, steam or boil the sweet potatoes until tender. Preheat the oven to 200C/180C fan/gas mark 6. Drain the potatoes well and mash with the butter. Spoon on top of the meat, sprinkle with the cheese and cook on the top shelf for around 20 minutes until golden and bubbling.

STEP 6

Alternatively, cover and freeze the pie or mini pies for another time. Defrost thoroughly before cooking - you can do this by leaving it in the fridge overnight if you like. Preheat the oven to 200C/180C fan/gas mark 6 and cook for around 30 - 35 mins or until golden, bubbling and hot throughout.

Easy peasy risotto with chilli & mint crumbs

Prep: 5 mins **Cook:** 45 mins

Easy

Serves 2

Ingredients

- 1 tbsp vegetable oil , plus a drizzle
- 1 onion , chopped
- 3 garlic cloves , crushed
- 200g risotto rice
- 1l hot chicken or vegetable stock
- 300g frozen peas
- 25g Italian-style hard cheese (pecorino, parmesan or vegetarian alternative), grated
- juice and zest 1 lemon
- 2 slices leftover bread (a few days old is best)
- 2 frozen red chillies (deseeded if you don't like it too hot), see tip, below left
- small bunch mint , chopped

Method

STEP 1

Heat the oil in a large pan. Add the onion and cook for 5 mins, then add the garlic. Stir in the rice for 1-2 mins, then add the stock, a little at a time, stirring continuously until the rice is nearly cooked and the stock has all been absorbed – this will take about 20 mins. Meanwhile, tip the peas into a colander and run under the hot water tap until defrosted. Drain well, tip into a bowl and roughly mash with a potato masher.

STEP 2

Remove the risotto from the heat, stir in the peas, cheese and a squeeze of lemon juice, then season well.

STEP 3

Grate the bread on a box grater into chunky crumbs. On the finer side of the grater, grate the chilli. Heat a drizzle of oil in a frying pan, add the chilli, lemon zest and crumbs and cook for 2 mins until crispy, then add the mint and sprinkle over the risotto before serving.

Really easy cheese fondue

Prep: 5 mins **Cook:** 8 mins - 10 mins

Easy

Serves 6

Ingredients

- 125ml white wine
- 450g gruyère, grated
- 450g cheddar, grated
- 50ml kirsch
- 1 heaped tsp cornflour
- small baguette, torn into chunks, to serve

Method

STEP 1

Heat the wine in a heavy-based saucepan, then add the cheese, a handful at a time, and keep stirring. When all the cheese has melted, add the kirsch, followed by the cornflour, stirring until completely smooth.

STEP 2

Serve the pan in the middle of the table on a wooden board with the chunks of baguette for dipping.

Easy cheese & onion slice

Prep: 30 mins **Cook:** 45 mins

Easy

Cuts into 8-10 slices

Ingredients

- 600g baking potato, peeled and chopped into chunks
- 300g mature cheddar, 200g grated, 100g cubed
- pinch cayenne pepper

- large bunch spring onions, finely sliced
- 1 egg, beaten
- 500g pack all-butter puff pastry
- jar caramelised red onions (we used English Provender Company), to serve

Method

STEP 1

Heat oven to 220C/200C fan/gas 7. Boil potatoes for 15 mins until tender, then drain well and smash a little. Cool slightly.

STEP 2

Mix the cheese, cayenne and onions with the smashed potatoes and stir to make a mouldable filling. Roll out the pastry to a rectangle about 25 x 35cm. Carefully lift onto a baking sheet and brush all over with beaten egg.

STEP 3

Press the cheese mix along one of the long sides of the pastry, leaving 2cm pastry free on one side for sealing, and half of the pastry empty on the other side for folding over later. Fold the pastry over the filling and press the edges together, before trimming with a knife and sealing well by pressing the edges with a fork.

STEP 4

Brush with egg and bake for 30 mins. Cool, then slice and serve with caramelised red onions. Can be made 1 day ahead

Easy ratatouille with poached eggs

Prep: 15 mins **Cook:** 50 mins

Easy

Serves 4

Ingredients

- 1 tbsp olive oil
- 1 large onion, chopped
- 1 red or orange pepper, deseeded and thinly sliced
- 2 garlic cloves, finely chopped
- 1 tbsp chopped rosemary
- 1 aubergine, diced
- 2 courgettes, diced
- 400g can chopped tomatoes
- 1 tsp balsamic vinegar
- 4 large eggs
- handful basil leaves

Method

STEP 1

Heat the oil in a large frying pan. Add the onion, pepper, garlic and rosemary, then cook for 5 mins, stirring frequently, until the onion has softened. Add the aubergine and courgettes, then cook for 2 mins more.

STEP 2

Add the tomatoes, then fill the can with water, swirl it around and tip into the pan. Bring to the boil, cover, then simmer for 40 mins, uncovering after 20 mins, until reduced and pulpy.

STEP 3

Stir the vinegar into the ratatouille, then make 4 spaces for the eggs. Crack an egg into each hole and season with black pepper. Cover, then cook for 2-5 mins until set as softly or firmly as you like. Scatter over the basil and serve with some crusty bread to mop up the juices.

Quick & easy party nibbles

Prep: 30 mins **Cook:** 30 mins

Easy

Ingredients

- See recipe method, below, for all the ingredients you'll need for your canapés

Method

STEP 1

Bloody Mary shots with horseradish: For 10 shots mix 700ml tomato juice with 50ml vodka, juice from 1 lemon and a good splash of Tabasco and vegetarian Worcestershire sauce in a jug. Season then chill. To serve, pour into 10 shot glasses, add a thin cucumber stick to each as a stirrer, and top with a small spoon of creamed horseradish.

STEP 2

Quails' eggs with sesame dukka: Toast 1 tbsp each of cumin and coriander seeds and 85g hazelnuts, then whizz in a food processor until finely chopped. Mix with 50g sesame seeds and salt to taste, then serve in small bowls with 24-36 hard-boiled quails' eggs, halved, alongside for dipping.

STEP 3

Mini avocado tarts: Buy mini croustade cases from the supermarket, then put a small spoonful of sour cream in each case. Finely dice ripe avocados and mix with a little lime juice, some poppy seeds and finely snipped chives, then pile on top of the sour cream.

STEP 4

Parsnip chips with maple-mustard dip: Peel a parsnip per person, then cut into chunky chips and roast with sunflower oil and seasoning at 220C/200C fan/gas 7 for 20-30 mins until crispy and golden. Mix a 200ml tub crème fraîche with 2 tbsp grainy mustard, 2 tbsp maple syrup and some seasoning and serve the hot parsnip chips alongside for dipping.

STEP 5

Halloumi dippers with chilli pineapple salsa: For the salsa, finely dice 200g fresh or canned pineapple and mix with 1 finely chopped red onion, 1 finely chopped red chilli and juice of 1-2 limes to taste. Use a 250g pack halloumi per 5-6 people, slice into chunky strips, thread onto small soaked wooden skewers and grill, turning, until crispy. Serve with the salsa.

STEP 6

Greek kebabs with houmous & tzatziki: Cook and cool bought falafel, then skewer each one with a chunk of cucumber, small cube of feta and a cherry tomato. Serve with pots of houmous and tzatziki on the side.

STEP 7

Crunchy poppadoms with mango chutney: To feed a crowd, finely shred 3 peeled carrots, dice ½ a cucumber and finely slice 4 spring onions. Mix together with a squeeze of lemon juice and 1 tbsp toasted mustard seeds. To serve, pile into bought mini poppadom crisps, top with a small dollop of mango chutney and scatter with coriander leaves.

STEP 8

Fig & blue cheese skewers: Skewer wedges of fig and cubes of blue cheese onto small cocktail sticks or skewers, then drizzle with a little runny honey and scatter with thyme leaves to serve.

STEP 9

Christmas pudding truffles: Melt together 200g dark chocolate and 200ml double cream, then crumble in 100g leftover cooked Christmas pud (buy a vegetarian one), then chill. When firm enough, use a melon baller or roll into balls, then dip the tops in some melted white chocolate, scatter with edible decorations, then chill to firm.

STEP 10

Mini cranberry & orange scones: Knock up a batch of scone dough (from a packet or find recipe on bbcgoodfood.com), adding some dried cranberries and orange zest into the mix before stamping out 4cm rounds and baking. When cool, split and spread generously with orange or jaffa curd (we used Waitrose) and top with a small dollop of clotted or thick double cream.

RECIPE TIPS

HOW MANY TO SERVE?

As a general guide, for a two-hour party serve 6-8 nibbles per person; for a four-hour bash – 8-10 nibbles per person and for an all-evening event – serve 10-12 nibbles per person.

Easy elderflower liqueur

Prep: 20 mins

Easy

Makes 750ml

Ingredients

- 8-10 heads of elderflowers
- 100g golden or white caster sugar
- 1 lemon , zest removed with a peeler, ½ juiced
- 750ml vodka (reserving the bottle)

Method

STEP 1

Snip off the long green stalks of the elderflower, leaving enough to hold the flower heads together. Gently rinse the flower heads in water and check for bugs.

STEP 2

Push the flowers into the emptied vodka bottle or a jar, tip in the sugar and leave for 1 hr.

STEP 3

Add the lemon zest and juice and vodka to the bottle until it is completely full with no air space, keep any excess vodka to add back later. Seal and leave for 48 hrs. You can leave it for longer, but the flavour will change – it won't necessarily taste more elderflowery.

STEP 4

Pour the vodka into a large bowl through a fine sieve (use muslin or a coffee filter, if you like). Add any remaining vodka, then pour into clean, sterilised bottles. *Will keep for one month.*

RECIPE TIPS

USE THE RIGHT JAR OR BOTTLE

Don't use a bottle or jar that holds more than 750ml – there should be no room for air at the top once the vodka is poured in with the elderflowers, or the petals will go brown.

ADDING THE SUGAR

You can add the sugar towards the end of the process, if you prefer, to control the level of sweetness. To do this, you need to make a syrup. Add the sugar to a small saucepan with 100ml water and bring up to a simmer to dissolve the sugar. Leave to cool, then stir into the infused vodka in step 4. If you prefer a sweeter result, make more sugar syrup and add it.

www.ingramcontent.com/pod-product-compliance
Lightning Source LLC
LaVergne TN
LVHW070815281224
800066LV00014B/1011